Y0-BVO-035

THOUGHTS ON
FREEDOM

Two Essays

Lorin McMackin

BJ
1461
.M39
1982
West

SOUTHERN ILLINOIS UNIVERSITY PRESS
Carbondale and Edwardsville

Copyright © 1982 by the Board of Trustees, Southern
    Illinois University

All rights reserved

Printed in the United States of America

Designed by John DeBacher

LIBRARY OF CONGRESS CATALOGING IN PUBLICATION
    DATA

McMackin, Lorin.
    Thoughts on freedom.

        1. Free will and determinism—Addresses, essays,
lectures.   2. Liberty—Addresses, essays, lectures.
1. Title.
BJ1461.M39   123'.5   81–23297
ISBN 0–8093–1076–7   AACR2

Contents

Preface
vii

Alternatives and Restrictions
3

Choice and Determinism
69

Preface

TRADITION HAS ARRANGED that my title be misunderstood. Such is the common penalty for the use of a common term. The offended word is to me plainly best, so I persist; but despite practiced implication, my topic is freedom, not politics. Persons who have asked of my writing or have seen its beginning presumed at once that I intended an explanation of or polemic for my approach to utopia. I do not have one, here or otherwise, but the error is nearly required.

This does not assert that no mention of political systems follows. In much of the first essay, descriptions of them are indispensable, and references to these extensive as they relate to and illustrate our presumptive exercise of choice. Democracy is given more attention than most, not as attempted thorough or direct examination, but for the help it offers to the study of freedom.

I begin at the beginning of man's interest here, at the surface of the problem, with the concern that is the most troublesome to nearly any person, and at nearly any time for each of us. If the misfortune that befalls him seems inevitable, his reaction may be only disappointment, of whatever degree. If somebody did it to him, the emotion will likely be less simple, his sadness tinged with or dominated by anger. The added distress is not that if he stumbles he will fall, but that a human tripped him; not that if he fails to eat he will cease to live, but that someone destroyed his garden; not that a stream makes difficult his visit to a friend, but that her parents intervene, or that a prince forbids his travel. It is the level of human practice, what humans do to humans, singly and in groups. But the other fact remains, it underruns all we do. If a person sufficiently stumbles, he will fall; if he does cease to eat, for whatever reason, he will die. Streams do impede travel. And though princes and parents, for good and for bad, are often in the way, they are not necessarily so. They can also stand aside, or encourage rather than forbid. They both bless and damn. But the river can do only what it does; it cannot change itself. Whatever difficulties, conveniences, or delights we have with it are not its problems; good or bad, they are ours alone.

The second essay is given to determinism, the hope that all, in the full sense of this word, flows from the personal, conscious decisions of a perfect creator who transcends his universe, or the wish that all, again fully all, has been, is, and will be caused by the inherency of the self-existing universe, the relentless working of reckless, mindless matter. The topic suggests metaphysics; the writing does not. Of that which to me seems beyond knowledge, I presume to know as much as anyone does; but nothing is not worth writing of, it brings no content. Enough ignorance shows through even my best passages. A fantasy could be built, but that would be of little use save to the few who relish every opportunity for academic attack and embroidery. I am probably capable of no other philosophy than social; perhaps no one is otherwise.

A late draft was read by Professors James Diefenbeck and Richard Pratte. I thank each for important suggestions.

Alternatives
AND
Restrictions

ONLY BECAUSE OF ITS COMMONNESS, 'freedom' is a most strange term. It has been so honored, blessed, canonized, romanticized, publicized, labored, stretched, and loved that it has become for many persons little other than a weak near-synonym of 'the Good'. It has been so much the forced description of one, then another, and ultimately a great variety of social situations that often it seems only the label of some favored political arrangement. Our various "liberation" movements offer hourly attestation to this; other times have made other presentments. When we use a word so widely, we seldom use it well. But though usage is continuous and without meaning, usually without thought or even awareness, a little deliberation shows that 'freedom' is defined simply and with ease. It denotes the absence of restraint; its referent is the ability to choose. A person is free to the extent that he is not controlled; he is free when he can choose his action.

Dispute of this is common. We often find careful insistence that when a man can do as he pleases, his circumstance is not freedom but license. If, however, we inquire after 'license', we soon find that the act so-called is always an instance of freedom; it is only a freedom that is disapproved. 'License' is in this sense an unfortunate word that almost fails to stipulate a concept; we would likely be better without it, but we cannot avoid so common a term. To call an act thus is to confess a dislike of it, to say it is immoral; but it cannot be immoral unless it is free. A person who charges license is complaining not that an act was committed of necessity but of a freedom that should not be tolerated; his discontent is that a restriction has been violated or ought be imposed. No one so complains until he has been offended by an act that he believes avoidable.

We often hear that license is the abuse of freedom, but this is to speak far less than clearly. It can be such in only other than the intended meaning, only in that there is a conflict of freedoms, only in that someone's license, his freedom, abuses the freedom of someone else. But this too needs help. It is never the freedom, either of doer or of the done-unto, but the presumed restraint upon the doer—that which purports to deny his freedom—that is violated. Only laws and customs, only restrictions are transgressed. Only selves are abused. Any demand for an end to license is a demand for a limit on human action, a narrowing of somebody's opportunity to choose. License is not the abuse of freedom but abuse with, or through freedom. Only this or a similar formulation avoids the offense against language of a usage which insists that bad freedom is called 'license' and that good freedom is called 'freedom'.

The other side of this confusion is the implication that a person is free in only those actions in which he is restricted. If, as is often held, the condition, not of freedom but of license, exists for a person who behaves as he wishes, it follows that the condition of freedom prevails for him who is without choice. But no one who talks of license is thinking this far ahead. For him, an act chosen within the rules, or within what he thinks they ought be, is an instance of freedom; any behavior outside of law, or of what he would have it be, is license. He might even say if pressed that though the rejected act is as intended it is not part of or taken within freedom. Again, license is violation, and the desired state is called freedom. This conflict and shifting between meanings produces the near impossibility of distinguishing who is free and who is controlled, and of when and how each condition obtains. The breach of rationality is mended by the understanding that license is neither the opposite of nor an alternative to freedom, but an instance of the latter. License is alleged only when a freedom is in dispute. He who so condemns an act, necessarily believes it to have been chosen.

The definition of 'freedom' is commonly further obscured by the assertion that freedom cannot exist without restriction, from which is then improperly drawn the idea that it therefore cannot be the absence of restriction. Apart from its pseudo-derivative, the statement has two meanings; one is true, the other is not. If it means that freedom is dependent upon restrictions for its existence, that it can never be save there is restriction out of which it grows, the assertion is false. If it means that a human can never know immunity to all restrictions, that the experience of total freedom is impossible for him, it is correct; but this is to describe a circumstance, not to define a term. It tells us what is, not what 'freedom' means. Restrictions are necessarily upon something, something that would otherwise be unrestrained. They are not such absolutely; there can never be one that is upon nothing. A potential restriction always restricts something potentially. Without an ability of choice there could be no restrictions because there would be nothing to restrict, actual or potential. A condition that restrains us might exist undiminished if humans could not choose or if we did not live, but it would not be a restriction on humans. Restraints do not make freedom possible, but they are inevitably, constantly part of the human situation; any freedom that man has is forever hedged about by them. The point is not that freedom cannot exist without restriction, but that it does not.

The statement, "Man is never free," is then true or false depending upon what it means. If it says that he is never in such circumstance that all conceivable actions are open to him without coercion or inhibition, it is true; if it says that he is so constrained that there can never be an action that is open to his choice, it states that which our experience denies. The idea, "Man is never free," and its grammatic opposite, "Man is always free," are, properly understood, of the same meaning.

That the concept of freedom goes beyond experience and suggests an impossible state of being is a notion that some persons develop and then encourage themselves to be worried by. The objection is that the idea cannot be as here stated because life is not unrestricted, but this is to confound the definition of a concept with the description of a situation. 'Freedom' is not a synonym of 'life'. Its referent is part of experience, not the whole of it. Their confusion at the idea of freedom's being the absence of restriction is to conjure a vision of human life totally without restraint, then dismiss the definition because the fantasy is ridiculous. They distress themselves without cause. 'Freedom' has the objected-to characteristic in only the sense as does any other definition and only if taken in permanent isolation from other ideas, which would be stupid were it possible. It no more goes beyond experience than does a definition of 'human skin' which omits reference to the air that surrounds human bodies. Consistence would demand belief that the idea "squirrels have bushy tails" presumes that squirrels do not live in trees. Squirrels' tails come into contact with branches, leaves, twigs, and trunks and are modified thereby; but if we were to include the tree within the definition of 'tail', we would soon have to declare 'universe', 'squirrel', and all other terms synonymous. We would have not a language but a great collection of worthless symbols, every one of which conveyed the meaning 'everything'. Definition serves a single purpose; it attempts to set one term apart from all others that clarity be enhanced and understanding facilitated; it does not presume that reality is thereby altered or that existence ought otherwise be ignored.

Zero degree absolute has likely never been experienced, but it does not follow that 'absolute zero' means almost absolute zero. There can be reasonable doubt that any human has seen white, or if it be insisted, pure white, but it does not follow that, except in casual conversation, 'white' means light grey. 'Grey' is vague; 'white' is precise. If 'white' were to mean grey, almost white; and 'absolute zero' were to signify the presence of some heat, almost zero; both 'almost white' and 'nearly zero' would be without meaning. The qualifier is not helpful except that it is tied to a concept of definable precision. We need thousands of these ideas—abstractions and idealizations—that we may think about what we have known; then in a description of experience, any one of them can be qualified as we think appropriate. If 'freedom' could refer to only experience at large, only to the vague condition of being somewhat restricted, we would lose all preciseness of denotation, could never modify the term usefully, and would be helped, if we could have it, by a replacement word for the meaning that 'freedom' now carries. We need abstract and ideal terms not because we are amused by toying mystically with impossibilities but because only through them are we able to deal intelligently with the commonplace.

A discussion aimed at producing a definition of 'freedom' will almost without fail, if pressed far enough, eventually bring forth "Freedom is freedom with restriction," an apparent though unreal lapse of logic which makes the matter entirely clear. The word is used here in two senses, one strict, the other careless. We have only to ascertain the meaning of 'freedom' at its second appearance in this seemingly confused sentence and the problem is solved. Its first usage is merely inaccuracy which merits no further attention, except that in every such instance one should note its strong tendency to weaken the language. Obviously, in its second usage it refers to actions chosen, undertaken, and consummated without interference or compulsion, the power to choose, the absence of restriction; it can mean no other, for no other is left to it. The meaning of the statement is then that man's inevitable circumstance or some favored political context ('freedom', carelessly used) is such that his competence to choose ('freedom', precisely used) is always partially restricted.

I

OUR IDEA OF FREEDOM begins in the ever-present, apparently universal human experience of choice, of each person's being always faced, though never in his every event, with the necessity of choosing. Freedom, thus known, is a fact of human life that every society of which we have knowledge has recognized; none has been without some system of moral judgment. This characteristic of reality is then described, that it may be comprehended, by our mentally separating the idea of it from all others; and it is named, that it may be easily mentioned, with the name's being defined in accordance with the description of the object. Description is similar to definition, but it is of acts, objects, characteristics, events, scenes, situations, and other presumed facts, to whatever degree of narrowness is desired, rather than of terms. They are different classes of ideas and are arrived at by different processes—description, being of the fact rather than of our label for it, is often much more detailed than definition—but ultimately they become the same. If the definition of the word 'sparrow' and the description of the bird called sparrow are in conflict, at least one of them needs help. Though a word is our invention and can be used as we like, usefulness suffers if usage is confused. Through failure to match definition to description, noun assignment commonly can go awry in two ways, by using the name of a totality for part of it, and by applying the name of a characteristic of life or constituent of a circumstance to some broad social situation.

Both are injuriously common, and the latter is a major impediment to the understanding of freedom. In either case, usefulness is plagued by treatment's fault.

We intellectualize freedom with descriptions, and with definitions and a name, that we may know what it is and that we may speak and think deliberately, but the source of the notion is elsewhere. Here, rationality deals with that which is given in awareness. Intellectually, we believe that we are free because existentially we feel that we are.

That there is fact beyond the thought can be denied. Our experience proves that we believe that we choose, not that we do; it tells of faith rather than of knowledge. To claim that we are without any power of choice is to assert that which only a dogmatic determinist would affirm, but there are such about. There always have been. They insist, without proof, upon a posited condition of which we have no experience; that is why they are called dogmatic. Undeniably, we often feel restricted, but to enlarge this experiential fact into an explanation of everything, a universal determinism, is as ridiculous as would be inflating the fact of experienced freedom into a belief that we are totally unrestrained. This approach is not the one which determinism ordinarily takes, except in the most naïve apologies. Determinism is not an empirical derivation but a metaphysical faith; it is not to be proven but to be believed. The forces of determinism are not found in experience; they are not inhibitions and coercions that chafe upon us. Never are they requests which we resist, perhaps at our peril. They are controls that we never feel; paths that we take necessarily, with no recognition of their necessity; absolute orderings of life that never reach experience, no matter what their reality. Determinism is a painless condition, save that every pain is determined. It may be the fact of the world, but we cannot know that it is.

The idea is always in the back, and occasionally in the fore, of the human mind. It is an attractive intermittent notion to persons who are frustrated and, particularly so, to those who feel guilty; it relieves them of the responsibility for their problems. In this employment, it is a crutch rather than a commitment; one is less concerned in believing than with fooling himself. That done, he can go back to making choices. But it has often been an intellectual belief of insistent, though difficult, perseverance. Some persons want seriously to believe that determinism is real. Many try with assiduity, but the way is hard, and they toil much without gain. A person who consciously adheres to it will always, when attending to that subject, attempt to talk as though he has unshakable faith in the obvious, but he can seldom behave as though this faith exists. He seems always to be choosing, always to be acting as though he believes that he is choosing, usually to be talking as though he is trying to influence the choices of others, often others who are being deliberately obtuse. Perhaps, he is fated to do so. It is easy to talk occasionally as a determinist but almost impossible to behave in a convincing manner.

But however unlikely it may appear, however much life may seem to deny it, regardless of the extent to which it is rejected by men, determinism, carefully understood, always remains a plausible explanation of how and why we live. It may be extreme; it may seem undesirable; its believers may seem to be faking, but it is never implausible. No proofs can be raised for or against it; it just may or may not be.

But though we can never know that determinism is not, these essays are based upon the supposition—pretense, if it be wished (determined pretense?)—that man is faced with alternatives and has the power to choose among them. Else nothing can be done; nothing can be proposed; nothing can be speculated, for even the apparent speculations and our presumed opinions thereof can then be only as they must.

THERE IS COMMON ASSENT that freedom is good. All persons, in one way or another, admit to this faith. Democracy proclaims it; freedom is that system's apparent reason for existence. Tyrants strive against it, for it is always the first wish of tyranny's subjects, which force then has the first duty to put down. Conservative persons resist it; they are irritated that it changes the freedoms to which they have grown accustomed. Holy causes demand it as their self-evident right to control their members and captive potential converts. And our doctrinaire "Liberals" justify its suppression by appeal to its sanctity.

Here is also the motivation of persons who try to distinguish in kind between freedom and license. The former seems so good that they resist associating bad acts with it, cannot bring themselves to relate it to that of which they disapprove. To do so would seem equivocation with moral principles. Hence the spurious category.

Radicals of whatever political extremity are perplexed by freedom, as they are by everything else. Extremists never understand anything, except perhaps the uses of power. This is why they can permit themselves no doubts, why they are self-forced to the certainty that they are right. This is why they comprehend neither the problems that they attack nor the proposals which they push, why they see everything as intense evil or unmitigated good, why their solutions are always simple, regardless of the complexities to which they are addressed. This is why radicals shout rather than discuss, why they demand rather than suggest, why they can destroy but are incompetent to build. Even the most mature among them are incurable adolescents. They both love and detest freedom; they demand it for themselves and deny it to those whom they enjoy oppressing.

Slaves and serfs have particularly acute needs in living with the idea of freedom. Many persons of all classes are self-misled, but slaves and serfs are required far more than most to dissemble before themselves. Restrictions upon them are heavy and extensive; little is left to their choosing; personal wishes are not only ignored but are often punished simply because they flow from initiative. Slaves must be kept in their place and made to love both their condition and their masters; only severe and consistent repression can meet the need. The freedom of such persons is slight, so they crave it much—the apparently innate human desire to choose, augmented by deprivation. But what they want most, they can least have. That which is desperately wished for is wantonly desired because it is denied them, and, being denied, it is unattainable. They can save themselves only by deciding that this which is of first importance they do not want, else their lives are naught. Because what they lack is impossible, they turn to what they can have, which is only that which is forced upon them, and take comfort that it is best, for they have made it their desire. The attempt is only to find comfort in what exists. Rebellion is improbable; they are more concerned to justify their condition than to change it.

At all costs, they must escape warranted self-pity. We can tolerate self-pity, even enjoy it, when it is feigned, when it is only part of life, when we can see beyond it to something better that we can at least grasp for when we must, but never when it is merited, when it is all there is, when hope is gone. Self-pity is unbearable when it is real. The slave must contrive a situation in which he does not have to feel sorry for himself, in which he is relieved of the constant self-accusation of being a coward and a failure, of the continuing reproach that against his wish and with his acquiescence his life is being wasted. If to survive as a functioning being he has to believe that he is fit only to be a slave and that it is good that he be cared for by his betters, he will rejoice in his inferiority. If he is not given justice, he will make it.

The subjects of an absolute monarch behave in this manner when their ruler is overpowering in fact as well as name. In defense against themselves they even ascribe divinity to him. If they are weak enough, if they are so thoroughly controlled that they have no possibility of getting loose, they are ardent to press Godhood upon him. When they allow this human to beat them down, they are cowards and fools. But if they convince themselves that their repressor is God, they are simply doing their duty to the community and the cosmos; they are prostrating themselves before a higher being. In their frailty, they need to be cared for; in the extremity of frailness, none but a deity can meet the need.

But when the monarch becomes weak, his subjects throw off the notion that they are inferior; they do not need it, for the king no longer has the strength to be respected. They break into the palace, even into the temple, and capture God and kill him, for he is no longer God; he has failed them. They are not constrained so to call him when they are not weak; it is ridiculous so to name him when he is not strong. Their attack upon him is a complaint against the treatment which they have received, but also against his weakness, for it is this that destroyed their illusions and their comfort, that proved to them that they were wrong, that exposed them before themselves as craven and gullible. They kill him because they hate him, but less for what he did to them than for what they did to themselves; they could forgive him the former, but never the latter. It is not accidental that in most of the societies of our culture, and of the cultures associated with ours in earlier days, the most notorious attribute of God—our God, their God, any God—was his omnipotence, and that even now those who love Him most are those who are most persuaded of His Power.

Though slaves and serfs and some others may give the impression that they care little for freedom, though they deny, no matter how calmly or how seldom, that it is important to them, they show their desire in their steadfast resignation and, in a sufficient emergency, in their eager seeking after subjugation. The desire for freedom is their urge to reject it. Others exhibit approval in other ways, usually by direct affirmation. There is much surface confusion but little basic doubt. Persons assert freedom; societies thwart it; it is seen to be the basis of love and the motive for hate, the spring of satisfactions and the slough of frustrations, the essence of life and the source of sin, but there is near unanimity that it is good. Freedom is favored by the persons who dislike it. Those who claim to despise it, those who labor to put it down, do so because they want it for themselves. Those who claim to need it not, expect it to be exercised by others and in their deprivation assume that this is good. It is clearly a primal human value and a basic human wish.

MANY SOCIETIES HAVE GIVEN freedom official and public commendation. Ours may be the prime example. Of those we have known, none has been more concerned with the idea, none has used its name more widely. The word appears in nearly every political utterance of more than a few sentences; the concept is in all of our basic political documents of whatever length. Any group that is unhappy tells of this by asserting that rightful freedoms are denied it; any person who dislikes his condition claims that his are impinged upon. We often say in description, or in complaint, that this is a free country, and we are often distressed that it is less so than it ought be. Traditionalists complain that everybody else tries to steal our freedoms, and others are wroth that tradition withholds them. The word is used by candidates and by statesmen, in propaganda and in honesty, by wise men and by fools. It is always with us, like sex and taxes. Much of the usage is superficial and inane, but this shows how highly approved freedom is, else its name would not be taken for support.

So we are caught in what at first thought seems a ridiculous contradiction. Freedom is good, we desire it much, we are pleased with what we have, and we want it more. But along with this insistence, there runs another in the opposite direction. Every time a legislative body meets, we want more laws. Whether it be the federal Congress or a state assembly, even a city council or a school board, we want it to be busy and to produce many results, and without wasting time in argument. We are not interested in talk; we want bills approved, and many of them. But laws are restrictive; they tell persons what is required of them and what the penalties of disobedience will be. We love freedom; we want more of it for ourselves and our fellows, and we constantly demand a greater weight of restriction upon us all.

The usual suggestion at this point is that we need laws to protect freedom, which says something, but not well. If taken literally, it indicates that the more restrictions are upon us the freer we are and that complete freedom would arrive when we were fully controlled. Often it is put as: We restrict freedom to make freedom possible; or, we limit freedom that we may provide greater freedom. In some sense, this is true, but only in a most imprecise and less than helpful one. In the form here stated, the idea is a paradox, which simply shows that something is wrong in its formulation. It may be useful symbolically, but descriptively, it is confusion.

On the surface, we have an odd problem, but not

one of us finds it strange. It is common to the entirety
of mankind, the basic dilemma of human association.

II

IF WE SUPPOSE A SOCIETY that is consciously, deliberately, persistently dedicated to the belief that it exists
to make its members free, we have a means of beginning to comprehend the difficulty. If such society at-
tended not to the securing, maintenance, and maximization of freedom, it would fail its central duty and
lose its reason for being. It must form itself upon the
premise, certainly not the only one, but this the basic
ideal, that the first purpose of its existence is to provide, increase, preserve, and defend the powers and opportunities of individual persons to make choices. But
after it comes to this commitment, it has yet the problem of how to organize itself.

The least possible thought gives us immediately
the obvious suggestion. First thought often has little
else to recommend it, but at least it presents the obvious. The understanding among persons that would
permit the greatest personal freedom would be one of
no organization whatever, that none should exist. Organization is repressive, laws are coercive, society
binds; they are not to be tolerated. Government is
abomination. No man can read another's soul; none
can know another's good; no legislator, no judge, is so
wise that he feels the urges from which my actions
grow, that he foresees the goals that I intend, that he
discerns my waking hopes, my midnight uncertain-
ties, my frustrations, my loneliness, and the depth of
my need to hate and to love, to nurture and to kill. My
rights are mine personally, not copies or imitations of

those of other persons, not those of humanity that I share by participation. They are not privileges that I take by privilege from a public storing place. They are begat and born in me; they are mine alone. As I am unique, they are unique. The common right is the right to be uncommon, the right to be unmolested by mankind's corporate striving to keep me small and sterile, to make me hateful and cringing before myself, the right to unoppressed, unchaperoned life freely lived, the only climate in which the human spirit can expand and flower.

This is the commitment to anarchy. It is a romantic notion; it easily degenerates into a sentimental one. Verbose emotional extravagance is its usual ornament. As romance, it is often a counterinfluence to the extreme of control; by calling for the alternative to government, it helps keep political commitment open to discussion. As sentimentality, it merely disturbs the world with its noisy sniffling.

To many persons this seems too refined; the term is almost always used less cleanly. A body of customary, perhaps called "natural," law of interpersonal relations which everyone is obliged to obey, and to which conformity is exacted by private enforcement, organized and otherwise, does or does not constitute government, depending upon what definitions are contrived. But it is beyond argument a control system of appreciable effect and performs an important function that every government takes on, usually as first task. It is often called anarchy, but only upon a large concession to reality. Were the need here a practical minimum of social control, I could adopt the foregoing or suggest a more structured plan, and some would call that, too, anarchy. But my purpose is elsewhere, so the description is unmitigated by practicality. The need is formal and illustrative, not evangelic. The one needs clarity; the other can be inundated by it.

The only requirement of the extreme formulation is that there be no social control, of whatever style it may take. Laws, regulations, customs ought not exist. If anyone protests that such condition is impossible, all must agree with him. Empirical perfections are not available. Total anarchy cannot be had. But this does not disqualify the idea; it only qualifies the practice. Anarchy is a concept, an entirely satisfactory one; it has no internal conflict, it is fully thinkable. It is the ideal limit of a continuum; here it is pure. Practice is inevitably mixed. Full anarchy is possible as principle, never in society. It is by definition the absence of society; there are no forms, no systems, no controls, only autonomous persons in unsupervised interaction. If there is no interaction, the concept is irrelevant; an isolated person is in neither society nor anarchy. The principle is amenable to practice only as goal, only as a standard against which to test circumstances. A society can strive toward it. One society can be judged more nearly anarchistic than another. Every society is somewhat so; it may be near to or far from the ideal, but it is necessarily on the continuum.

The recommendation is that to ensure the maximum possible freedom to its members as persons, a society attempt to achieve the least possible organization, that it forbear enactments and promulgations and discourage the formation of customs. The temptation at this point is to specify that only necessary controls be permitted, but this is easily misleading because the common usage of 'necessary' employs the word in an instrumental sense, as in a statement that some act or thing is necessary to the attainment of an end. In this sense, there are no controls that are necessary to anarchy; none are needed; they are all not only dispensable, they are all evil. The only meaning of 'necessary' useful here is that of inevitable. These must be allowed simply because they cannot be disallowed. Even then, they are not permitted, they are tolerated, and this, on theory, temporarily. Probably the best that can be said is that inevasible restraints are suffered in transit.

Each person is free of restriction imposed by custom, by law, by government, by society—on theory, entirely so—in practice, nearly and increasingly so. A simple statement says it all: social controls do not exist. No policeman will interfere with him, no court or regulatory agency will call him to account, no legislature will take notice of his behavior; these too do not exist. He can do as he pleases.

First thought has given its suggestion. Most persons upon further thought reject it. All are attracted to being untouched by social controls, to having no needed worry for a neighbor's thoughts or a warden's care, but each is disturbed that all others would be likewise unhindered. Scarce is the man who relishes being repressed and driven, but scarcely can any avoid fear of the other hundreds, thousands, or millions that social pressure will not urge to conformity. The plan will not suffice. It leaves every person completely subject to whatever effect can reach him of any act that any other person, all others individually, wishes and is competent to perform. As each is free to do as he pleases, so is every other member of his anarchy. The problem is interference among persons. This is objectionable to nearly everybody, so why not just be rid of it? Let us abolish interpersonal conflict. Such can be done in imagination and approached in practice.

Man can be an egoistic and useless creature, but he can never be happy when he has lost his way. In this unnatural condition, his confusion is commonly so great that he can imagine no cure for the illness save the aggravation of his infection. In single-minded, insatiable drive, he demands to augment his already hopeless autonomy and insists upon casting off even the few remaining threads to the source of his guidance and comfort. Satisfaction is impossible for him; he can never get enough of that which he has never needed. But he thinks to ease his wretchedness by distending its cause, and he drives on to press license into perversion and perversion into insanity. Often he can be brought only by force into cooperation with his purpose and larger self, but this is needed only when he has been long shut away from proper authority, and his passions, intelligence, loyalty, and hopes have therefore fallen into corruption and disarray.

Man is a social being; his life is the life of his group, of his community, of his society. He finds his satisfaction in the tasks that are assigned him and his gratification in the pleasures that the social system puts in his way. The happy man is the ordered man, the disciplined man, the one who is properly subservient to a larger whole, the one who knows his place and his function. Miserable is he who grasps after privileges; he wastes himself upon illusion and cannot enjoy even that which comes to him. When he serves only himself, he does even this badly. If not corrected, he will soon in bitterness be howling after "rights," and he will hate both himself and his fellows.

It can be variously stated and applied to many circumstances, but man has basically only one right, the right of each person to immerse himself in service to the common good as this is decided to be by the common power. The social organism commands its members as a man does his. Conflict between the two thumbs is unthinkable; each has its tasks; each keeps its place; neither dominates the other, nor wishes to; they work independently and together for the whole. Interference between them is pathologic; it results only from failure in the organism. The basal right is therefore the right to do one's duty; in this, all must be free of impediment. Society is thereby served; its needs are met. The person, too, benefits, for in duty he discovers his path; in the performance of duty he finds his salvation.

Such is the other end of the continuum. It is the totalitarian view. Government is complete. Persons are important because they are the social structure, but for no other reason. Each is important because he is part of that structure, but independent decisions are not made. Sacrifice for the common good is universal practice. Every person knows his tasks, those of his associates, and the expectations for each. He knows when to step forward and when to stand back. He knows when to give way, when to hold the door, and when to be unmoved. Each is aware of what is required and what is denied. The primary commands are the requirements. If he always performs the required, the need to refrain from the denied never arises. No act is merely permitted; it is either demanded or proscribed. The rules are complete; the plan is full.

This can be set out with as much force and vigor as can anarchy, but the need is for calm, cold intensity. It is not a romantic idea. Commitment to it in such style is possible; passionate ignorance can be met anywhere, but to give it a romantic presentation is self-defeating. The nearly necessary result is effusive sentimentality that is immediately repulsive, just as a statement of anarchy in classic, restrained language seems merely fraudulent. The one is exuberant foolishness; the other, stilted triviality. Both are laughable—for a person not to offended too be amused. The imperious, almost ascetic locution that a recommendation for full government is best served by easily slips off into pedantry, in which form it bores all upon whom it intrudes, but an austere, skillfully presented call for totalitarian society can be chilling—or inspiring, depending upon one's needs and doctrine.

The emotion with which this position and that of anarchy are ordinarily presented and contended for is essential to them. Each is an extreme attitude; it is difficult to maintain. It ignores much that experience has shown to be important. Life never lets us see it clearly and is forever contriving examples of its converse. Doubt is severe and, if permitted, unremitting. Hence comes much of the tendency to evangelic work, which offers two great benefits for the believer. The fervent, repetitive recitation of doctrine that proselyting requires is strongly supportive of steadfast belief; he who delivers such is usually more stirred by the speaking than his audience is by the hearing; the inspiration and reinforcement fall primarily upon him.

But beyond and through this routine though useful effort occasionally there occurs a supreme moment. Nothing will put doubt so well to rest, for a little while, as the making of a convert. In this is not just common help, not just support for the ordinary day; it comes full-laden with reward. Now his anguish, his persistence, his pride of doctrine, his sacrifice and his tears find joyous vindication. He was right, after all. There is another to stand with him, one whom he helped to be born again. In this new believer, he is justified and reassured; in his miraculous responsibility, he may find new strength. He feels the cleansing of his faith, the slipping away of the sins of filthy doubt. All of this is his, but only for a little while. Soon his need is great again. As some say, God will never let him rest. The emotion is necessary; it helps keep harassed commitment closed to unwelcome thought.

The totalitarian concept is often asserted as a model for practice, but no one has claimed that it can be imitated whole. It too is an ideal. This is why every attempt to create a society that would be its shadow is based upon penalties. If faultless creation were achieved, punishment would be unknown; every person's behavior would be perfect, perfectly in accord with social standards. But though perfection is not possible, it can be approached in the sense that one society, regardless of by what degree removed, is closer than are others, in that any society is closer at some time than at other times. It is a goal that has been often deliberately striven toward. Total government can be thought; we can entertain the idea, but it is a principle that is not amenable of execution. In any society, it is a useful standard of judgment, for every society is on the con-

tinuum between the pure, perfect, unattainable, but
easily conceived forms that are its ideal limits.

The first recommendation is the first thought of
nearly everybody. The second seldom occurs openly to
anyone. The former is immediately credible, though
naïve in the extreme. Restrictions interfere with freedom; laws and mores are restrictive; if there were no
social controls, everyone would be free. The latter at
introduction seems eccentric—that full government
provides freedom is at first thought too implausible to
merit a second—but upon familiarity is recognized as
equal in plausibility and naïveté to its alternative. If
someone blocks a street, others cannot use it or must
remove the barricade. If my house is burned, I lose my
possessions, my home, my shelter and much time. If
someone breaks my arm, I suffer pain and inconvenience, perhaps permanent injury. If a man is killed, he
loses his existence, and with it his power of choice.
Such outrages can be controlled by government; arson,
battery, murder, and blockage of a public thoroughfare
can be declared illegal. If these laws are then enforced,
we will be less troubled by dastardly, arrogant, and per-
fidious acts. Interference among persons is restrictive.
Government reduces this conflict. If every act were
subject to the rule of law, we would all be free.

Most persons find also this unacceptable. They
have little objection to predictable behavior by their
fellows, to knowing what to expect of even a stranger.
They are pleased to be secure in their persons and in
their families, friends, and possessions. Few are unhappy at the prospect of surer knowledge of life's future than any other system allows. But they cannot believe that freedom is attained through the abolition of

opportunities to choose. Even if they could, that freedom they would reject; they want to make choices.
They will not assent that they would be desirably free
if they had no permissible alternatives, if the ever-
present single pair of options were to obey or disobey.
Further, nearly every one fears government. Persons
are powerless here, but society is ready for immediate
action against a member and is without limit. This
plan too will not suffice. The massive weight of government that it lays upon each citizen is intolerable to
all save a very few of us. But repudiation of the totalitarian concept places that of anarchy in its stead.
There is no other; a continuum has only two ends.

MAN IS IMPOSSIBLE TO PLEASE. All that is is put aside
as evil. At one extreme, each is free of social control
but fully at the mercy of every other person. At the
opposite, he is clear of interference by individual others but completely subject to the whim of society. At
each pole, he is completely free and fully restricted, at
one extreme in one manner, in the opposite at the
other. If he has the freedom that anarchy allows, he is
freed of pressure by society; if he has the freedom that
government provides, he is freed from interpersonal
conflict. Or, the same concept in alternative wording,
he may have the limit that anarchy permits; if so, the
actions of others, not only those designed for him but
many more as well, impinge upon his. Ill will, bad
will, good will, and the best of will find him with and
without intent. No authority can be called in defense
or even to urge his fellows to help him in his need. He
stands or falls alone—humbly, in degradation, in dignity, perhaps in nobility—but alone. He may have the

limit that full government imposes; if so, he lives by
the plan and command of the sovereign power. Social
decisions reach him as assignments to be performed,
conferments to be accepted, and often, be he so remiss
as to have any, negations of his secret hopes. In any
objection he raises, in any nonconformity, he is again
in isolation, reviled in his act, suspected far beyond it,
and without help. He can call no friend to his side; he
stands alone, if he stands at all, against the social mass.
Each of these freedoms is had only with its corresponding restriction. The restriction and the freedom that it
provides, or the freedom and the restriction that it produces, are inseparable because they are identical. Each
of the freedoms is its corresponding limitation; each of
the limitations is its correlative freedom. They are but
two manners of naming, of thinking about, a single
fact. Anarchy and total government are each one idea,
not a pair of separable ones.

There is no way out. Every society is inextricably
caught between these apparent evils. Any political organization has only two alternatives, each of which is
distasteful and in no more than part avoidable. Because
each pole is undesirable, we try to stand away from it,
which takes us closer to the other. We dislike each, so
we choose both. Thereby is attained a mixture of
goods, which is to say, of evils. This we often call 'democracy'. The term is apt because only at some remove from both poles can the members of a society
exercise any control of it. Democracy is a mixture of
anarchy and corporate despotism. It is not that which
we might best like; it is just the best that we can do.

Man is impossible to please, not because he is perverse, irrational, irresponsible, or stupid, but because

what he fully knows he wants and would enjoy is not provided by the world. He who would be sane must bring himself to appreciate the circumstance in which he lives, and live with rather than against it. Occasional complaints, frequent struggles, and continuing difficulty are expected; life is hard, and complex. But a career of crying out against metaphysical "injustice" is profitable only for him who relishes unremitting frustration and requires inevasible defeat. He who will live efficiently must know the human situation and relate his actions to it. Learning to do so is not easy; it is our major social difficulty and one of the several that fall primarily, though far from entirely, upon adolescence. Perhaps this explains in part the affinity that children who are striving to become adult have for romantic simplicities; perhaps in this period of strain, reality is too much to be accepted whole. But we who learn insufficiently are individually chargeable with perversity, irresponsibility, stupidity, or worse, which show usually in excesses of arrogance, ambition, callousness, and greed.

This is not as any man would have it, if our wishes ruled the world. We all can dream a more pleasant arrangement, more agreeable each for himself alone. The condition most desired by everyone, our continuing urge, is to be simultaneously clear of both restrictions. Every child knows this; he will try to create it when he can. No one is long among adolescents without finding the boy who, at a meeting in a doorway, says, "Get out of my way; this is a free country," and an hour, a day, or a week later, when the circumstance is reversed, says "I don't have to get out of your way; this is a free country." He is trying to have the interpersonal situation both ways; socialization is not easy to come by. Our wish is to abolish the restrictions while retaining the benefits of each. It is a good dream, entertaining and well loved. The will to tyranny is strong in all of us.

Only a tyrant can experience the fact, and even he only in dilution. He can seldom walk alone among his subjects unless he has become God, and even a deified despot is engrossed to keep his retinue always before him. This perfection, too, cannot be had, but some have grown old and many died young in trying. The proprietor of a society is served by social control but not bent by it. He uses law and custom against others while standing aside from both to exercise anarchy's freedom among subjects made docile by inertia and fear. As he is successful, neither society nor persons stop his path.

The fantasy is often less well structured, less entangled with reality. Let foolishness be unchallenged, and the dream can be extended to every man; let all be free of both restrictions. Now each person can impede every other, and all are beyond interference. We cannot even imagine the situation. There is no point to tyranny if there is none to exploit; slavery is harmless if no master can reach us—such trifles may be amusing, but they are irrelevant to the world. There can be no universal tyranny, no genteel, superficial, soft tyranny for sensitive ladies and gentlemen, in which everyone gains and none is hurt. Tyranny can be only personal; it is either real or nonexistent.

Most of us reject the urge to free ourselves of all restrictions not through dislike but because this condition is in one form impossible, in the other impractical and, if we wish, immoral. To be unrestrained remains desirable, but there can be only one tyrant in any situation; no one wants it to be someone other than himself. Tyranny can be attractive to the potential ruler, occasionally even to an actual one, but seldom to anyone else; few wish to become subjects. The prospect for ambition is slight. The work is onerous; the risks are great; failure is easy. That the rewards of one's even unbounded effort will be conferred upon another is ever probable. The responsibility of attempting is heavy; of succeeding, near to unbearable. Few of either group die in bed, save of slow poison or lingering wounds. And he who lives has himself to face; he has the reviewing of his mistakes; he has the reliving of his moments of cowardice and foolhardiness when judgment or courage failed ambition and his best chance was lost; he has the constant renourishing of his abiding hatred for those whom he has wronged and of those who have outdone him. Not many of us have the combination of strengths and weaknesses, needs and fears, that such life requires; most who do never find opportunity to test them. So we learn to refrain. Tyranny is rejected in guilt and in righteousness, in weakness and in strength, from fear of others and fear of oneself, in rationality and in passion. We desist, perhaps sadly, but bitterly only if we are fools. We must take account of the world as well as of our ambitions.

Anarchy puts every man at the whim of every other. Full government never permits them to choose. Tyranny subjugates each unless he is the master. All are intended for freedom, the latter for that of one only, the others for the freedom of each. But none is acceptable by mankind. Argument can be raised that one or another ought fervently be desired by all, but this falls far from the point. None is commendable by the provisional criterion that society exists to make its members free; none is admissible by nearly any man's subjective standard for his personal freedom. None of these will do. All that remains is the confusing mixture of goods—and in every detail simultaneously of evils—which like every other social system is never better than it must be and seldom does as well as it might.

III

DEMOCRACY IS PROBABLY a peculiar concept. We who have lived with its conspicuous presence throughout our lives usually think it only natural. We may be right, but overpresumption is easy. Everyone other than a lifetime hermit has had experience of it; it has always been, though often only to slight and unintentional extent, part of every society. But it is a middle-range idea that is difficult to grasp and is little understood even by most who have loved it much and have lived much with it.

The practical range for social existence between the ideal limits called anarchy and corporate despotism provides for and encourages much variation in practice. Escape is unimaginable, but movement on the continuum is easy, even unavoidable against the most stubborn resolve. Here every society, in spite of its wish and best effort, finds its home. Here we all are caught. Throughout most of this broad practical range, in all save the extremes of it, democracy is possible. Therein, always uncomfortable and dissatisfied, always restless, it moves, searchingly and precariously, always toward one of the evils—or, if more pleasant manner be desired, away from the other. Here, as often, the difference between optimism and pessimism is in the words that we use.

SOME ATTENTION DIRECTLY to continua will advance the explanation. Commonly, a continuum is represented visually as a line. This is adequate to most purposes but will not suffice for the present because it does not allow distinguishing among types. It wants breadth. The diagram needed here is the rectangle, which permits to be shown the various manners in which two qualities relate.

One of these modes is the blending continuum:

Here the two qualities are so mixed at every point other than the poles that they are independently indistinguishable; only the mixture is experienced. Each modifies the other, to the extent that each is present, with the result that neither is known separately. If the qualities are black and white, the continuum will range, except for the poles, infinitely through strengths of grey. If the poles be red and white, the remainder of the range will be infinite shades and tints of red, or shades of red and tints of pink, if preferred. If they were blue and yellow, there would be a smooth progression of greens, from the least greenish of greenish blue through the least greenish of greenish yellow. An excellent mechanical illustration is the single lever faucet—two supply pipes, one spigot, and one control. If the lever is at the far left, water is delivered from one pipe only, that which leads from the heater. If it is in the opposite position, water flows from the other pipe only, water that has not been through the heater. Each end is pure in that water is obtained from one pipe alone and is as hot or cold as the system provides at that time. At any of the infinite intermediate settings there comes mixture, ranging from an infinitely small amount of hot mingled with cold, through equal parts of each, to an infinitesimal portion of cold mingled with hot. We can imagine such device connected to water on one side and alcohol on the other, or lemon juice at one pipe and cider at the opposite. In every instance, the resulting blend is such that its constituents are not experienced separately and will rarely, and only with special intervention, be resegregated.

A second type is the canceling continuum:

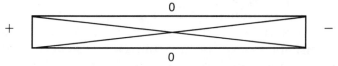

In this, any amount of either quality neutralizes, destroys, or converts a specific, not necessarily equal, amount of the other, leaving none of either that went into the process. There is no mixing of qualities because whenever they are brought together, all of at least one disappears. Chemical action is often of this sort, though the substances involved are usually discontinuous one to the other. If we think of the poles being hydrogen and oxygen and of so bringing these gases together that bonding occurs, no point will con-

sist of both. If the measure be the atom, at one-third of
the continuum length from the hydrogen pole there
will be neither. All free gas has disappeared; in its stead
is water. Rather than a mixture, we have a compound,
a substance rather than a blend of substances. At all
other points than the poles there is also one free gas; at
each of the latter, a free gas only. In diagram:

If we neglect the water, which by definition we must,
the conditions of the continuum are satisfied. Much of
the behavior of positive and negative charges, presumably dichotomous each to the other, is similarly describable.

A further pattern is the maintaining continuum:

Here is neither canceling nor blending. The proportions change, but the qualities persist in individuation.
Instances of each are always independently discern-
ible. Many illustrations of this are so common as to be
simple to the point of being simpleminded. A bucket
of paint in use is one; first it is full, then gradually
becomes less full until empty. A continuum of sand
and shot is another, as is one of apples and lemons. In
the former, the qualities are always segregated; there is
no confusion of fullness and emptiness. In the latter

two, mixing can and probably would occur, but the individual instance—the apple, the lemon, the shot, or the grain of sand—can be identified. Reseparation is achievable because the qualities are ever distinct. We can mix oranges and elephants, but we can still find the elephants—and, if they are careful, the oranges.

Tradition prescribes that the poles of a continuum be called positive and negative, the presence and the absence of a single quality. The practice is useful enough in abstraction that it be preserved, but we need use care against being blinded to its conventionality. The alternative to something is almost never nothing. Further, we create situations in which it cannot so be even by stipulation, wherein we deliberately state that both ends are presence; in a sense, both are positive. Black may be the absence of reflected light, and white the want of pigment. Blue and yellow are neither lack of the other, or each is. The choice of emphasis is ours. We speak of positive and negative electricity, but exchange of names would serve as well. The continuum of the full and empty pail seems secure enough, but this shows only that our concern is with the paint. If we want the bucket full of air, if we pour out the paint for need of a container, empty of paint is plus and empty of air, full of paint, is minus.

The distinction required in assigning a situation to the first or third of these continua is often as much related to our perception as to anything inherent in the circumstance. Qualities can be as much results of human sense as of anything belonging to its supposed object. If we were so small that we could be among the particles of color on a printed page as we can be among the furnishings of a room, a mixture of blue and yellow might be just that, blue objects and yellow objects. Secondary and modified colors might be impossible for us except at considerable distance. If our sight were so dull that we could not distinguish things smaller than ourselves, blue plums and yellow plums in mixture might appear a green mass. This is not deficiency or superiority; not occasion for shame or pride. The world is for us what it is because of what it is and what we are as part of it. We are of exactly the right size and have ideal senses for perceiving that which we perceive. The categories and assignments that we make are for ourselves, not for the convenience of some presumed being of radically different size or one of perfect perception, whatever that might be fantasized to be. If such exists, it will do as it can and needs. We do for humans; we can do no better than the best we can for us.

AT LARGE, MAN'S SOCIAL SYSTEM is a maintaining continuum, the third of those previously mentioned, though without the clarity of its empirical examples. In any society, the control pattern is some indefinable, at best amorphously ascertainable, point thereon within the range of possibility. Estimation of position is insecure; measurement is not to be considered. We have this:

government

anarchy

The extremes are the pure, unreachable ideal limits. Elsewhere is mixture, most of it available to the strivings of humanity. We can call this the continuum of social control or the continuum of interpersonal impingement; it is either, and it is both.

Social experience is a great number of interrelated but separately describable incidents. The description is neither necessarily made nor, when made, the single, unavoidable outcome of the experience. It can run in divers ways, as observation, purpose, need, and interest will have it. Description can organize certain particulars into a statement of the act or acts of one or more persons, it can speak of an event that bore or bears upon the same or other persons, or it can combine these into a report of cause and effect. It is necessarily arbitrary; all that it does can be done variously. This is not to imply that it is dishonest or careless; such can be but are not important here. Description is of happenings that were observed, that were of sufficient interest to observers that their attentions were drawn, that seemed to them of enough import to be worth remembering or reporting, worth setting off from experience in general. Other persons likely would have had differing sensations and made other judgments.

Diversity is inevitable, but with and throughout it we find also much similarity. This is only to be expected; we differ among ourselves, but we are all human. It is argued much that each of us is unique, which is probably true if each be considered whole. At least, in default of proof, this seems the safest guess, but so to argue would never occur to anyone not struck by our likenesses. It would not attract such passionate adherence as it sometimes does were it not such a small truth. Likewise, each description, taken entirely, may be unique; whether or not, variety is obvious. But in almost every one, each of its parts is similar to those of many others.

Through recognition of these similarities, we form classes of events. If every description were unique in its every part and in every sense, categorization would be impossible and probably unthinkable. The lack of similitude would leave each event a class of itself and any control, corporate or private, of social experience impossible. There would be no expectation; nothing that had happened could happen again. But this ability to form classes allows us anticipation. As need provides and competence permits, we define classes of actions that interest us. We are then often in position to decide what influence if any is to be exercised over future instances of them. Most are for the most part ignored, but some become vital concerns, and many others cathartic obsessions, each briefly held in bright intensity and quickly passing into foolishness, disrepute, and oblivion.

Human acts can be permitted, required, or forbidden. Those permitted, through either intent or neglect, fall to anarchy; those required and those forbidden are the content of social control. At our every expectation of human action, we have potential need for deciding what we want, whether events shall be at the wills of individual and competing persons or subject to efforts by social interposition to shape them for the common wish. Every roadway intersection offers its example, as does every other point where humans meet. We must judge whether a person may go through the intersection whenever and in any manner he pleases, at whatever risk to himself and others, or if order will be imposed to ensure each a relatively safe and convenient passage at his appointed time. We need judge for each class of situations if nearly every person can be trusted with his fellows' well-being, or if each must be forced to respect society's notion of it. We must decide how much if any of a person's comfort and weal is to be provided and how much if any will be defended by society.

THE CRUCIAL FACT HERE, the point that is almost universally overlooked, is that there are two distinct forces of restriction bearing at all times upon every social being. His situation is not that of freedom against limit, or as sometimes said, freedom versus oppression—the latter word spoken with a sneer—as though the topic were Good opposed to Evil. Freedom is morally neutral; so is restriction, limit, repression, whatever it be called. Only instances of them can be judged. I can be free to mutilate my neighbor's wife, rape his preadolescent daughters, torture his little sons, tie him by the neck, and burn him alive in his house or to give myself to the defense of persons who are so threatened and to the relief of those so afflicted. I can be free to commit certain actions or to interpose myself in the like actions of another in attempt to provide, through his not being free from restriction that he is unfree so to behave. A society may leave men free to perform its heinous acts, or it may coerce them that they refrain. Save as seen in the self through the will to tyranny, to be free is never in principle good. Moral worth cannot be appraised in other than the actual or potential particulars of its exercise.

What man is faced with, rather than freedom

against restriction, is restrictive force opposed to re-strictive force, or in a loose sense, freedom against free-dom. Basically, man has only one freedom, the power to choose, but this limited by two human forces. Therefore, it is possible to speak of two freedoms, one in negation of each of these restrictive forces, that is, freedom from interference by persons, each acting for himself, and freedom from social control. In this sense, there can be two freedoms, but in each, restriction is upon the single power of choice. We can then speak imprecisely of the social continuum as the continuum of the two freedoms, but it is strictly that of the two sources of limit upon the one freedom.

The central and inextinguishable social problem is knowing how much we want to restrict each person that we limit his impingement upon others and bring him to cooperation with whatever is seen to be the common good; or, the same idea in converse, how far we are willing to leave him free to do as he can and cares in spite of the cares of others. There is no point carefully toward which to set direction, no goal to strive toward save whatever vague and changing no-tion of need and virtue its time supports. The social continuum is not a guide to action; it gives no help to any judgment.

A society's preference, or whatever is thought it ought be—the common good, as it is often called—can go to any extreme or moderate demand. It can require priests upon the building tops, offering yet beating hu-man hearts to heaven, for the common good. It can re-quire that persons be assigned to make constant prayer, that the Deity have without let our acknowl-edgment of His Greatness, for the common good. It can create a plan of electoral government, and encourage citizen participation therein, for the common good. It can hold that two persons not more than ten feet apart in a quiet place must converse together, on penalty of being thought unmannered, for the common good. It can insist that every self-killed body be dragged by a hate-screaming mob to a country crossing, there to be interred in mean ground with a stake through its heart, for the common good. These and all others that human practice can invent are perpetual nominees to the public's commitment. The social continuum will not help us decide.

Neither will democracy so inform us. Beyond encouraging, to whatever degree of insistence, adherence to the faith, no form of society entails the laws and customs that its followers ought live by. These are the products of persons; they vary in time and from group to group. They are socially devised, not bound in the form. Pure anarchy and full government, though unavailable in practice, can be had as principles; thus, each points clearly in a favored direction. Democracy offers us not even this. It is a much more complex and difficult arrangement. Pure democracy is not a concept; nobody can imagine what it might be. Democracy is mixture without inherent direction; purity is inconceivable.

A first protest might be that the midpoint of the continuum is where full democracy is reached, but there can be no reason to suppose that a society fifty percent governed is more democratic than one governed to a lesser or greater extent. This guess will not do, but a more careful one arises next which tries to put perfection on another base. It suggests that as democracy is the government in which the governed govern, total democracy would be achieved if the governed governed totally. Every decision made within the society would be made by the society through referendum. If a person wished to scratch his nose, a vote would be taken to decide if he would, but prior to this another polling would have ruled whether or not it itched, or if he would recognize the discomfort. In an appendectomy, referenda would be required throughout not only to control whether or not the operation would be performed but to decide each step in its execution and, before that, of the diagnosis. Nothing would be left to persons, either as centers of will or as experts; the people would rule. We would have totalitarian democracy. This may seem a contradiction, but it need not be. Nothing in the bare concept of democracy requires individual decisions; the only necessity is individual participation in social decisions. Full democracy is simply total government; every choosing becomes society's choice. That most persons would find this distasteful is no threat to it; the validity of an idea is independent of its being loved. 'Democracy' is not a substitute word for 'desirable'. This fullness of shared decision making could never become fact; nobody would have time to do other than vote. The mass of details to be decided would quickly become unmanageable; then with no one doing anything but voting, there would eventually be nothing to vote on. That done, the exercise in futility could start again, if some yet lived. But this does not destroy the concept, we are looking for an ideal limit, not practical reality. However, as all decisions are to be made socially, each person's every vote must be dictated by vote; it too is a social decision. With this, imagination fails; the idea falls into infinite regress and has to be abandoned. The point is not that democracy is not a concept—it plainly is—but that the idea of purity is irrelevant to it. An ideal limit cannot be had; we have only a variety of practical limits that preference may choose among. There can be no full democracy in practice; there can be no perfection of the idea even in principle.

Political representation is not the theoretic problem here that it is sometimes thought to be. Representation is primarily a convenience, but one that makes democracy practical. To put every social decision to vote of the populace in even a small, relatively anarchistic society is temporal impossibility; no one would be able to meet the demand of franchise. All voting would become superfluous because no one could perform the decisions of the electorate, or, for want of voters, most referenda would perish as the price of accomplishment. Choice would then lie between extinction of democracy or acceptance of representative government.

That a practice is necessary says nothing to its being democratic, but instruction is had by noting in this case an important relation: representation is irrelevant except to democracy. The extent to which citizens are represented in any other sort of society is the extent to which that society's principal political commitments are modified by democratic practices. In tyranny, in total government, in anarchy, representation is out of place because in none of these do the governed rule. There is no point in giving even indirect formal political voice to mere subjects or to ungoverned autonomous persons. Representation is an unavoidable means to a society's being self-controlled; beyond this, it is a convenience legitimate to the extent that it is desired by those who use it. No lack of democracy can be ascribed to a decision, democratically taken, that stipulates other decisions will be made within policy by appointed or elected persons, if that authority can be retrieved by the same process. To ascertain weights, lengths, and capacities by popular vote rather than by careful measurement is undeniably democratic and indisputably foolish. To select competent persons, publicly accountable for their honesty, to perform and report the measurements is equally democratic in itself, though it reduces the number of occasions for voting, and is far more likely to serve the social good. The only basic problem in representation is when to apply it, when to compromise between principle and reality.

Democracy can exist anywhere within the broad central range of the continuum from a vaguely specifiable point near one pole to a vaguely specifiable one near the other. It can tend much toward anarchy or much toward government. It can utilize relatively extensive social control or relatively little. It is no more democratic, no more successful, at one point than at any other. It is not better in principle near one extreme than near the opposite. Perhaps its most obvious characteristic is that it is never still. We constantly try to balance anarchy against government, but it is never done; the fulcrum never stops moving, for the fulcrum is our corporate taste, which knows no home because it refuses to make one. No sooner does it apportion events to its presumed liking than it finds the arrangement unsatisfactory. Everyone holds that social control and the lack of it should be kept in balance, but

each of us calls balanced the situation which he thinks
would be to his liking. The movable fulcrum is a useful deception in concealing from oneself that he attempts to mislead others, but the self is usually the
only one fooled.

THIS SHIFTING AND SAMPLING about the continuum,
though of often important effect on persons, is for the
most part harmless to the democracy, but not necessarily so. A society can go too far in either direction;
the democracy can be lost over either end. When a society approaches so closely to one of the poles that it
can no longer practice the political process, that it can
no longer receive in orderly fashion the wishes and
opinions of its members, democracy is gone from it. It
has moved so far to extremity that it cannot bring itself back. It has lost itself in abdication. Democracy
can be ended by entirely democratic means; it can be
voted away in change of law or allowed to die through
alterations in other controls, either by social disinte-
gration such that referenda and elections cannot be
conducted or given effect, or in society's becoming so
structured and extensively formal that each person's
every vote is prescribed and therefore superfluous.
Throughout most of its range, democracy has power to
take itself back from danger, but when it approaches
too closely the pure form of one of its constituent
evils, it is trapped and society forfeits control of itself.

Major fads are particularly treacherous. A slowly
developing trend can be somewhat understood, even
controlled; it is open to intelligence; it can be criti-
cized when current. But when a people, or a significant
portion of it, seizes upon a notion, calls it good, and

demands the immediate purification of itself and every person, an urgency is often engendered that precludes care and thought. Society is carried off in one of its two directions. Other causes, dormant perhaps, wishing to go that way join the drive in hope of free rides, prod it along, and profit from interest by association. Events move rapidly; attitudes change quickly. Yesterday's derisive hyperbole becomes tomorrow's settled virtue and unquestionable right. Standards of long-enduring moral judgment are lovingly commandeered if useful and dismissed as banes on human existence if not. Institutions, beliefs, mores, and persons that impede the path to revered utopia are damned in mass with the fashionable terms of deprecation and found guilty of keeping bad company. Persons whose need flagrantly to conform is onerous, who must make show of their respectability, who have great but vapid guilts that must be exorcised, and who are impelled to demonstrate their high morality join the movement, use its blessed words, assume the correct postures, produce the approved actions, wear the uniform, are seen in the proper places, and put themselves in the forefront of virtue, far enough ahead of the trend to move it further and more rapidly, far enough ahead to assuage all self-doubt of their sincerity. To be in style is more important than to understand; hysteria becomes a public moral necessity.

It probably will end suddenly, collapse into boredom and disgust after a great emotional release and be no more, but its danger is not therefore ended. The reaction to foolishness is commonly more foolishness. Extremity is often followed, seemingly challenged, by further extremity, in the opposite direction. A series of such swings, each greater than the one before, can fling society over the brink at one end or the other. Which one is of little importance. To come over either is usually to fall irrevocably into tyranny.

BOTH RESTRICTIVE FORCES are always with us, but in a segregated manner that we need precisely to understand. Lack of clarity on this point spreads confusion far beyond it. Each citizen is always subject to whatever social controls function in his society, though he may not at every moment be acting or consciously refraining under one of them, and is always available to be impeded or imposed upon by the unrestricted acts of others, though he may not at every moment feel their effect. But in the simple instance, he is reached by only one. He has either the restriction and the freedom that government provides or the restriction and the freedom that anarchy permits; he cannot have both. Each is always with him in his life at large and in the usual complexity of any moment, but in the simple instance, only one can be. A particular act is either governed or ungoverned, not both. Either law or custom commands behavior at a described event or neither does. The restrictive forces are mutually exclusive; they exist simultaneously and thoroughly intertwined but never for the same simple event. Any life, the complex situation of any person's moment, the society at any time is a developing composite of interrelated simple acts, some subject to social prescription, some not. Either the people decide, or persons do.

In the social continuum, the continuum of the two restrictions, the qualities are maintained in individuation. Each simple event and every class of such events, each of which is either controlled by society or left to anarchy, retains its identity. Movement on the continuum is achieved by changing the proportions of the qualities through the shifting of a class of events. Such class is taken from the quality to which it has been assigned and placed with the other. The society is thereby moved away from the pole of the quality that is thus reduced. Whenever a new law is given effect, a new regulation is promulgated, a new custom becomes binding, enforcement becomes more rigorous, or persons obey more readily, government increases, society moves closer to the totalitarian pole, and persons have more freedom from each other and less from the people. Whenever a law is repealed or comes to be ignored, when a regulation is rescinded or allowed to lapse, as enforcement becomes lax, as courts become less effective, or if persons obey less readily, anarchy increases, society moves away from the totalitarian pole, and persons have more freedom from government and less from each other.

In a very important sense, the amount of freedom, and therefore also the amount of restriction, is constant, it varies only in kind. At any point on the continuum, they are at one hundred percent of possible, ranging from entirely that of government through all mixtures to entirely that of anarchy. Both are constant from point to point. Freedom and restriction are always commensurate; there is always as much of one as of the other, in full and in kind. They can be the same concept. But though all points are equal in this formal and limited sense, their being infinitely various in quality makes them far from equally attractive at any time to any person or society.

There is another important source of diversity. Even when otherwise alike, societies seldom utilize the qualities of the continuum in uniform manner. We can imagine two societies at the midpoint, therefore qualitatively alike in being fifty percent governed, but each the converse of the other in distribution of social content. Every event that the one leaves to anarchy is in the other subject to social control. They are the same in one respect, opposites in the other. Even beyond this, uniformity would seem a miracle. Control can require or forbid; it may command in full or with exemption of person, time, and place. Societies are then formally alike in that each corresponds to a point on the continuum and has one hundred percent of possible freedom and restriction, and vary qualitatively in having differing proportions of the qualities, or kinds, of the continuum, and in content in having various distributions of events to the qualities. They are formally alike and differ qualitatively and in content.

The possibility for social variation is infinite on the one scale and at least inexhaustibly large on the other. Here a human penchant comports well with the part of reality to which it is relevant. We are never satisfied; some improvement always seems needed. Even a society that tries to be static has to contend with change. Newness creeps in against any resistance; some derives from forces beyond the society's power, and there is always the priestly demand for return to the ways of the ancients. Change is difficult for those who hate it, vexing for those who accept it with tolerance, and unmanageable for a society that craves it, but it ever is.

THE SOCIAL PROCESS, the development of the social environment, is fundamentally one of simple exchange.

The reference is not to persuasion and compromise among persons; these happen, but are not the topic. The referent is a procedure far more basic. Any interpersonal situation, if it be defined far enough, calls upon us to be limited either by corporate force or by persons each acting for himself, never by both. There is an enforced law or there is not. The intersection is equipped with a traffic signal or has none. Custom directs action or is lacking. Adultery is closely defined and proscribed, it is broadly defined and proscribed, it is loosely defined and ignored, it is given another name and required, or the concept does not exist. Examples could be endless. Usually there is some disagreement, but if a situation is sufficiently pleasing, we will wish it continued. If dissatisfaction is preponderant, we may strive to change it. Most basically, there is ever only one alternative to the existing arrangement; we can replace anarchy with social control or the latter with the former. We can adopt a law or create a custom or we can repeal a law or abandon it or custom, or we can through a great or minor change make either more or less restrictive. The trading is not among citizens but within the continuum. We replace, in a recurrent situation, a freedom of one quality with the corresponding one of the other.

There is a class of exceptions. What limit arises from anarchy if head scratching be permitted in private? What freedom is granted by government if it restrict or prohibit such act? We would strain after insignificance to find either. Imagination can contrive circumstances in which we might easily do otherwise. Some years ago, the abandoning of a can or bottle at the place of its emptying or of an automobile when it would go no farther was thought harmless. That the act was inhibition on anyone was not supposed; therefore, that governmental or customary prohibition or limitation of it would enhance anyone's freedom was likewise not considered. Now our attitude is changed; we strive somewhat to allow everyone freedom from trash by restricting everyone's freedom to dispose of it. Conditions have changed; our opinions have too. In other instances, changed attitudes have given constant circumstances altered value.

Always we live with many acts the occurrences of which society takes no note. That they happen may be well known; they may be important to persons, even life-dominating if thwarted; but in the corporate view they are trivial. These are not the events that society decides to leave to persons, but those not thought worth bringing to decision. If, concerning them, society chooses, it chooses only to be concerned no further. A behavior is an exception to every freedom's being also a repression if it does not in its content or produce gain the attention of society and if its prohibition would not reduce interference among persons. It is an extreme, not of the continuum, but of the trivial; though only at a time and only for society.

In all other situations reciprocity prevails. We limit the freedom of anarchy, to drive wherever on the road that we wish, in exchange of the freedom of relatively unimpeded travel. We forego the right to drive on the walkway, that we may be freer as pedestrians. We relinquish the freedom from criminality that close police surveillance provides, that we may be less bothered by being closely watched. When a situation is well liked, it is popularly thought an exercise of freedom; when it comes to be disliked, without its changing in any way we call it oppression. When what was considered a freedom comes to be looked upon as restriction, the tendency is to exchange it for the converse restriction, which will then be thought a freedom. Each is both, but we like to be free, which is tautology; we like what we like.

Each person wishes to exchange that which is a freedom for someone else and a restriction on himself for a limit on the other and a freedom for himself. When, however, their places are reversed, he may think differently. A person who is both a pedestrian and a driver, a hunter who has been shot by a hunter, a rapist whose beloved daughter has been raped, may have equivocal sentiments. We lose that we may gain; whenever we gain we lose. When we gain a freedom, we lose a freedom and a restriction and gain a restriction.

This returns the paradox of earlier mention: We limit freedom that we may make greater freedom possible; we restrict our actions that we may become free. As literal statements, these are nonsense. Not only does the pretended idea contradict itself, it cannot even be understood; there is no way of ascertaining that any freedom is objectively greater than its converse—on theory, they are equal. But intepretation saves it. We exchange one freedom not for one that is objectively greater but for one that we want more, one for which our wish is larger. It is greater only in its being more desired. We trade, for one class of situations, an ordering which we think that we dislike for one we hope that we will better like. But this is for stipulated persons at a moment; tastes vary from day to day and from man to man. Another time may see another wish; other persons may aspire to a different virtue or convenience. We choose in a class of instances to be limited, not by persons, but by social force which attempts to minimize the impingement of persons one upon another. For a different category of acts, or at another time, we seek restrictions, not by society, but by the interference of person with person that minimizes social pressure upon us each. From this chore we never rest, and always act in hope of being better pleased.

IN ANY BRIEF PERIOD, the relationship of the citizen to government and tradition is indistinguishable in democracy from that of any other middle-range society. Always is the combination of social controls and personal impingements, but what they are tells nothing necessarily of their origin. That some intelligent, respected man approves of, even is enraptured by, a particular mixture of freedoms does not indicate that its social context is democracy; that he disapproves of or even is offended by another does not show its home to be undemocratic. Democracy or any alternative, though the product of society, is not produced by the control mixture. Democracy or not, murder may be punished or condoned; society may be peaceful or violent; sex may be abomination or delight, perhaps both; traditional religion may be honored with pietistic fervor, laughed at, or ignored; marriage or policemen can be respected or despised; tort or libel actions may be easy or difficult to win; criminal trials can be formal games, attempts at the ascertainment of truth, ritual dramas of society's abdication, or demonstrations of governmental omnipotence. The source of interference, corporate or private, is independent of social type; any middle-range control mixture can be produced in any middle-range society. 'Democracy' is not a substitute word for 'well-liked'. That it is often thus misused shows how easily persons become enamored of, can even bring their worship to, a pleasing word, how many will cast it about at large and never forfeit innocence of its concept.

Democracy is society's freedom to choose its freedoms. In any other type of government, the control mixture is promulgated by a monarch, by a ruling party, by a church, by long-continued enslavement to tradition, or by some other outside force. Such society is not sovereign; only its proprietor is so blest. Hence, the democratic options are not of persons severally but of the social group, in which persons severally participate. The urge to make this personal is the will to tyranny, which in modified form is simple criminality. There is the desire to make judgments for classes of events and to impose these upon society or to decide in individual instances and attempt the evasion of law or custom, either the usurpation of the control of society or the violation of society's controls. The aspiring tyrant and the felon are of the same sort; the one is just more ambitious and perhaps more talented than the other. Political crimes and personal crimes, those against society and those against its members individually, differ otherwise only in how much they are intended to capture.

In democracy, the people, that is, persons collectively, decide what freedoms, and therefore restrictions, persons will individually bear. The same result, whatever the result, could be attained by a dictator's decree, but would rest upon only his wishes rather than the pooled judgments of his subjects. Any arrangement can be established by fiat, but only a decision of society can, save by coincidence, perform the collective will of persons. Only democracy provides its citizens the freedom to participate in social decisions; except contingently, no society provides any other. It is, most strictly, a freedom of society rather than of persons, but one, which because of its requirement for social decisions, necessarily extends to society's members.

Custom has provided that nearly anyone who reads, writes, speaks, or hears the term 'society' is in danger of misleading himself. Long-persisting and respected practice has so tangled this word in metaphor that meaning and referent are easily lost in fancy. Because they are usually hidden, they are commonly overwhelmed. Often we consider such as "Society has learned a punishing lesson; it has seen and grieved over the result of its errant foolishness, has felt and been made afraid by the heat of its passion, has been humbled before its enduring values, and has now, forsaking delusion, steadfastly and in penance assured itself that folly will not again become its guide, that its recent shame and sickness will not come again upon it, but that henceforth it will hold ever uppermost in spirit, thought, and action its historic dependence upon eternal law." Expressions of this sort are harmless if we are cognizant of what they are. They ascribe human characteristics to society, as though it were endowed with emotion, sense, and mind. This is, when well done, helpful pretense for honest reasons. It is not to be thought descriptive; it is not to be taken literally, even if the writer or speaker fooled himself. Everybody knows this, but usage is so pressing that effort is needed to keep awareness constant.

The aphorism that there is no society, only persons in society, is salutary here. It reminds us that in an important sense, society does not exist; it is an idea formed because of its usefulness. Society is not an entity; it is a process. It has reality only as does my mind, my circulation, my metabolism, my voice, or my stride. No action is ever taken save by persons. Society of itself never does anything, can never act directly. Only a person can act, but he can do so for himself or as agent of the corporate process or a subgroup thereof. A society can have human characteristics only by imagination, only in figurative speech. There is never, for instance, a happy group, though there may be groups of happy persons. Only the latter can be happy, sad, intelligent, or whatever; neither groups nor processes have such possibility. Society is not conscious; it does not think; it does not decide; it does not dispose. Persons choose to act collectively, then conclude what the collective attempt will be. If the action is performed, it is borne by agents who act individually for persons collectively. An executive officer is a person, a legislator is a person, a judge is a person; but each, as surrogate of the corporate process, acts for that which itself can never act. His functions he performs himself, but as agent rather than as principal.

Society is the system of relationships among persons. Whenever humans interact, there is to that extent society. In a secondary sense, it may be the group of persons in interaction. 'Society' is a name of a process and perhaps of a corporate group; it is never the name of an organism or of a personal being. A like concept but, in this respect, less subject to confusion, is 'democracy'. Democracy is one type of society, one class of relationships among persons. Any set of social interactions is democratic if the social process at large produces the control mixture.

There would be instruction here for radical anarchists and totalitarians, if they were not so extreme as to be incapable of learning. The one group urges us to hunger after a nonsystem of interpersonal impingements that never creates process; the other commands our subservience to the superior mind of organismic society. Neither hope takes account of reality.

An aphorism, too, calls for a little care; though not as much as metaphor requires. It is a brief, striking oversimplification that draws heed to an insight. While saying both too little and too much, it points the way. If it does this, enough is done; precision is not its office. It is important if it points in an important direction. Clarity of detail and fullness of explanation can come elsewhere. It has much the purpose of metaphor but is less esoteric, far more open to the uninitiated. The assuming of a metaphor to be literal is an act of ignorance, or of habit, but to receive an aphorism literally is an act of stupidity. The latter is usual only if the aphorism becomes a slogan, for then men will believe in spite of facts, and it becomes a fool's device. Exceptions become instances of evil rather than of elucidation, obscenities to be hid from public view. When discipleship advances to stewardship, the apostles make full truths of the master's part truths, precise dogmas of his hyperboles, and slogans of his insights. Foolishness is honored and ignorance carefully encouraged, for in a holy cause stupidity in the evaluation of doctrine is prized above all save obedience. It can be a calamity, but it does not happen often. Nearly always, an aphorism is taken as intended. Only a little care is needed.

THE SUPPOSITION UPON WHICH the preceding chapter generated, that a society might take as its first purpose the maximization of the freedom of its individual members, can now be understood. In that it is a fruitful starting point, heuristically valuable, it needs no modification. It is tenable as premise because it is useful; no more can be asked of it. More importantly, no more can be assigned it. It is not, cannot be the beginning place or the first duty of democracy. A society governed by its members is dedicated not to the enlargement of the freedom of persons but to the attempted satisfaction of their corporate wishes. The former is logically impossible, the latter is merely difficult. That we are fond to use the name of the one to identify the other does not bring the unattainable within reach.

Any social system has necessarily to take account of freedom; it is part of life. Democracy has a unique relation with it, the freedom of persons to participate in social decision. But this participation is instrumental activity, not final good. The democratic privilege of persons is necessity for such society; it is the means by which social decisions are society's doing, by which cooperation produces a corporate consequent. But it

has no value as end; only its results can be so honored.
Not many citizens would be serene to exercise con-
tinuously the political process entirely for the sake
of decisions that were not, could never be, carried out,
that were not intended for implementation. But this is
the distinguishing characteristic of a final good. It is
not intended for anything; no man has a purpose for it.
To suggest otherwise is like asking the usual person
why he wants to be happy. There will be no answer, or
a ridiculous one. It is as wondering what a committed
Christian wants heaven for. He does not want it for
anything; he has no use for heaven. It is goal, not way
station. Empty decisions will never be unknown in political endeavor, but we have not heard of the person
who would make them the reason for living, or a cause
for dying. Democracy is an instrumental good. Its
value is its process, not its existence; and, beyond this,
in its accomplishment, not in its performance. Man is
a political animal, but not to unlimited extent. There
is nothing that can be the explanation of everything.

Thus then does democracy exist. It is a difficult
and perilous condition, an aggregate of opposing evils,
a process always in danger of extinguishing itself in
pride or in self-hatred, in wanton change or doctrinaire
preservation, in dogmatic institutionalism or a fit of
chastity. To be successful, to survive, it must respond
to the wishes, the needs, often the intensely emotional, briefly held whims of its members, and in re-
sponding always maintain enough government to keep
the anarchy from being widely chaotic and sufficient
anarchy to keep the government from becoming broadly
oppressive. It is that society in which the people
choose the freedoms that persons will exercise.

IV

THE INTEREST OF THE FOREGOING is almost entirely the social level of human freedom, the human restriction of humans. Concern has been with interactions among persons, with freedom in society, with the freedom of persons among persons, with limits in society, and, if we are careful not to give the term too much meaning, social freedom. These are not several categories but one with several names. Central are the concepts of law and custom, the content of what is often called social control. That these and their referents are universal among societies attests to the at least nearly universal belief that persons live among alternatives. To enact a statute, to adopt a constitution, to alter a law, to impose a penalty, to refrain from enforcement, to demand respect for a custom or to work for its change each gives evidence of faith in the reality of human freedom.

Let us acknowledge that foot traffic wears and dirties any floor, that the floor's maintenance thereby becomes progressively more difficult and its repair and then replacement eventually necessary, that the walking produces vibration tending toward destruction of the building and churns dust into the air for all to breathe and carry. The results are inconvenience, discomfort, excessive use of labor, waste of resources, and various sorts of filth. Why have we not then cultivated the customary attitude that good manners require, and if enforcement were needed promulgated a statute prescribing, that everyone walk at least four inches above the floor? The question is silly, but useful; the answer is important. Social control does not require the pre-

sumably impossible. Neither does it command the unavoidable. Common understanding is that anyone
whose blood ceases movement will soon die. Why has
not our culture, intent upon the sinfulness of suicide,
then taken care that no man will his circulation, or his
breathing or catabolism, to stop? Again the question is
ridiculous, but it is importantly illustrative. No matter how we may honor, need, or detest a real or imagined act or how much we may crave or loath its known
or fancied consequences, we do not order or forbid that
which seems impossible or inevasible. Exceptions can
be only apparent; they are instances of confusion or
malevolence. The concern of social control is avoidable possibilities.

Fundamental to the concept of enforced conformity is that every person who is subject to any instance of it is capable of disobeying, of acting athwart
the command. Social restrictions are in principle viol-
able. A law forbidding murder and a custom requiring
that every man remove his hat when in the presence of
a superior, such as a woman, presumes that man kill-
ing and head covering are optional, that they are acts
of choice. If the behavior were inevitable, prescription
or proscription would be merely foolish, for its being
merely fruitless. Embedded in every social restriction,
no matter how frightening or how gentle, is the belief
that it goes to an opportunity for human choice. The
social attempt is then to load the alternatives that the
choosing be influenced, that the approved act is performed or the disfavored rejected. It must entail belief
that in the instructed behavior humans are free to do
other than as instructed; free, not in the sense of having permission to disobey, this is explicitly denied by

command to the opposite, but in the basic sense of a condition that makes control achievable. Had we no freedom, we could honor no rule.

A social restriction is always of doubtful prospective effect. Laws can be broken; because they often are, we set penalties. Many are largely successful; others fail miserably, a few ostentatiously. Some are effective at one time and useless at another. Each is attempt, never assurance. It tries through disapprobation, malediction, ridicule, and threat of punishment, or less often by their opposites, to influence behavior. By making an alternative less or more attractive than it otherwise would be or by associating it in artificial and uncertain causal relationship with a presumably undesirable or desirable occurrence, we strive to teach ourselves to covet or to shun. Such as these are practical means; irresistibility is unavailable. A social restriction is an attempt to coerce choice among avoidable possibilities.

THE SOCIAL LEVEL OF FREEDOM AND LIMIT, or the faith that it is real, requires a level of restricted choice that underlies interhuman relations, one that is logically prior to and more basic than the actions of persons. That we are concerned with possibilities indicates that we recognize also impossibilities, else we would use neither these nor similar words. That some acts are thought avoidable shows that others are believed necessary. Many of them at the surface of behavior are socially contrived, but even these are most basically not of human origin, only of human use. Society can confine me within brick walls, but society does not create my being unable to pass through thick masonry or my inability to resist the force that carries me into confinement.

Seldom can I take the direct route from where I am to where I want to be, even from one room to the next. I cannot walk through the mountain; I go around, I go over, or I do not make the trip. I cannot travel directly to a distant city; the earth does not yield. I can want to; I can think of so doing, but the wish is not susceptible of execution. Streams, lakes, seas, stones, voids, dangers, hills, walls, and the sphere of the earth seem ever to be where I would like my path. The world, without which I could do nothing, for there would be nothing that could be done, constantly limits my doing and impels my being done unto. From each statement of what can be we infer something of what cannot. Gravity binds me and sets me free.

No human can fly. At best, he swims badly. He can fall well, but usually to his disadvantage. He can cross a supporting surface, but more slowly than he usually desires. I cannot leave my table tonight at 7:30, spend fifteen minutes in Chicago, and be back at work at 8:00. I may move from point to point only by passing through the intervening space. Nearly any adult can lift fifty pounds; none will lift fifty thousand. Nearly any person not blind can see a dog, but none can see a virus. All not deaf will hear some frequencies, but others will be heard by none. I cannot write this page in Italian, or Tocharian. I will not go to Mars this month. I can likely avoid stepping from a cliff, but if avoidance fails, falling will be necessary.

Here we have not encouragement to conformity, suggestions hopefully put forward, orders, threats, cajolery, and example, but that which the world provides. Conceivable acts are of three types: the avoidable, the inevitable, and the impossible. Thus are we presented with the physical level of freedom and limit. Life is lived among conditions that are merely what they are, not what humans make but that which humans find. We can be mistaken; we can misunderstand, but we live with the given, and die by it.

A physical restriction renders certain conceivabilities impossible, or, if alternative wording be used, inevitable. The distinction between the concepts is principally that of how an idea is stated; they are opposites and therefore closely allied. If I try to fly by a running jump from a cliff, I will not fly; I will fall. If I attempt to force myself into flight from a standing start, I will not fly; I will stay on the ground. All evidence suggests that no man will live forever; it is impossible. He will die; it is inevitable. "I will sever this steel girder with one bite." False; such is impossible. "If I bite this girder, it will remain whole." Correct; it is inevitable. There is always contrariety, but must be and cannot be are always related. Wording can change the polarity of such idea without altering its content beyond a quibble. The one set of restrictions is relevant to either version; the difference between them is superficial, but their sameness is basic. To assert either is to imply the other.

Unlike a limit of human origin, these are for us in no sense optional, but continuous and certain. They never attempt; do not command; cannot forbid, nor succeed, nor coerce. We do not resist; we do not obey; we do not defy. Obedience, proscription, defiance, and coercion are irrelevant to them. They are not appeals to the will. A physical restriction precludes the performance of an imagined act.

AGAINST THE PHYSICAL RESTRICTIONS we are, in the full sense, powerless. That they bear upon us always, always from beyond our reach, we know beyond doubt, but we know not why they are as they are. No human has ever changed even one; there is no prospect that a human ever will. Even so, the barriers and impositions of environment often hold us only partially helpless. The physical freedoms which give us our acts of choice, the avoidable possibilities, allow us indirect action to relieve against some instances of impossibility. If the need to pass through the mountain is great, perhaps we will make a tunnel. If so, I may then walk through the mountain. Not through the stone, that remains impossible, but through the air which fills a horizontal hole in it; I have always been able to do that. If moving directly from a point in one room into the next room is important, we can install a door. We then may walk, not through the wall, but through the doorway. The enticement of flying has long been so attractive that planes are built to do so. But if one takes me along, I will not be flying, that remains impossible, but riding in a machine, which humans have been doing for centuries. I cannot walk on water, nor swim nor jump great distances, but I can use a bridge or a ship. I cannot run rapidly or far, but I may find a conveyance that will take me one hundred miles in an hour, or a minute, though I move not at all relative to the surface that supports me.

We have these and thousands more. Others seem

potential. I will probably never stand on Mars, but the trip is likely for some. All came and will develop from using the restrictions selectively. These we meet in mass; each is always operable, dependent only upon the needed conditions to make manifest an instance of its effect. They are never altered nor overcome, but perhaps they can be manipulated. Circumstances can often be arranged for use to our intent. We change each time, not a restriction, but one or more conditions to produce a particular circumstance. In providing a platform to support an object, I do not overturn gravity; I utilize it and other restrictions that the thing stay in my place for it.

We distinguish two categories of impossibilities, the absolute and the contingent. If I am unable to go from one point to another because of an intervening chasm, stream, or wall, the impossibility is provisional; that I might walk on water, fly, or move among the molecules of granite is impossible absolutely. Perhaps the former can be remedied, but the latter will not be influenced. Building a bridge or driving a hole may require only sufficient commitment. No amount of unrelieved enthusiasm will radically alter my size, structure, or specific gravity. Absolutely, I am subject to the attraction of particles; contingently, I will fall if left unsupported.

Thus we expand freedom by increasing the range and diversity of avoidable, attainable acts. But this we never do apart from cost. Every physical addition subtracts something, for there can be no change that is only accession; it is also alteration of that which has been. We never merely add a bridge; we occupy space; we shade ground and stream; perhaps we alter the flow

of water or impede travel on its surface; we command
material that would otherwise be elsewhere. Whatever
is done, conditions are modified and other uses pre-
cluded. But we can with care provide desirable possibility exceeding that which is removed, and occasionally extend even the variety of alternatives. We are
often fooled and often foolish, and we often change our
minds, but progress can be had.

Thereby also is much of society's power achieved.
The conceivability of social control rests not only
upon the physical freedoms, which present and whence
derive our alternatives, but also upon the physical limits, for these provide the means to its enforcement.
Upon the possibility of utilizing impossibilities depend all penalty and threat of penalty. Walls and voids
confine; they can be constructed. Axes and knives may
cut; they can be provided. We command many ways to
death and pain, and are endowed to withhold ourselves
from whom we disapprove. Every punishment, severe
or mild, derives from our imperfect ability to apply
these and a few other impositions; to construct, hold
ourselves apart, and exercise irresistible force. They
grow from our freedom to use impossibilities to interfere with freedom. Both social control and interpersonal impingement—all that society permits, discour-
ages or stimulates, requires and forbids—all that
peoples and persons can accomplish are possible because we live in a physical environment that imposes
upon us both freedoms and limits.

Choice
AND
Determinism

THE ESSAY WHICH PRECEDES is concerned not with the source of choice but with the conditions of its exercise. Study has been on opportunities for choosing, on the operation of freedom among the restrictions of environment. These latter are of two sorts: those which arise from social activity, the human restriction of humans, in relation to which freedom reaches so far as it has uncoerced choice among possibilities; and those that exist apart from human action, the physical restraint of humans, in contrast with which freedom extends so far as it has the possibility, irrespective of coercion, of choosing among conceivabilities.

I

As CONCEPT OR REALITY, each of these and the combination of them is insufficient unto itself. Just as the social level presumes and requires the physical, together they imply and are dependent upon a further and more basic faith. Each creates alternatives, not freedoms; they provide, not the power to choose, but occasions for its employment. Hence the caution that the terms 'social freedom' and 'physical freedom' can easily be overloaded. The need is for choice as a constitutant of human existence, for the reality of an inherent human capacity or process that restriction can be upon. This quality is not a freedom of action that is created by arising opportunities but the persisting capacity to act if opportunity is presented. Granted human freedom, alternatives are of environmental origin, but the freedom that allows them to be such is independent of and logically prior to its environmental qualification. Apart from a human power of choice which supports them, there can be for us no avoidable possibilities and no social striving to control choices among them. Events will never offer options to beings who cannot choose.

It will be protested that a person is not free to act who is without opportunity to do so. Stated with this precision the idea is correct by definition, but it tells nothing of his ability. It describes the situation of the moment; it says only that he is contingently unfree. If the objection were recast as, "He is not free who is without the occasion to act," it would be defensible only upon interpretation; in this latter form, it confuses ability with opportunity. No one can play the piano if no piano can be had, but this tells of physical objects, nothing of skill and knowledge; it speaks of availability instead of proficiency. If in response to our asking a man if he can drive an automobile, we are told, "Of course not, I am not in an automobile," we would think him perverse. We asked of ability and were told something of location, an irrelevance to obvious intent. If I inquire of a person if he is a carpenter and am told only that he is a talker with me, I have been informed, after asking of skill, naught but of his current activity. That we have such words as 'competence', 'capacity', 'ability', 'proficiency', 'skill', and 'propensity' shows that the fictional respondents, and persons who would have us imitate them, misuse the language. Otherwise, there can be no efficacy that endures between uses, and we cannot properly think of Mr. Rubinstein as a pianist when he walks from his instrument, we ought not call Mr. Solti a conductor when he is traveling, and Mr. Chamberlain is not an athlete when in his dressing room. The concept of a sustained competence intermittently applied is descriptive of much of our experience; every human action is related to many such. The capacity for freedom must be one of these, a persisting quality of humans, the continuous competence to choose, else the presumed restrictions and alternatives of environment do not exist.

Abstracted from its operational setting, the power to choose seems absolute in several senses, none of which implies a mystical or rational, self-existing and/or perpetual entity; the concern is a human process. If, in thought, we separate this capacity from its application, we find that it is unavoidable. I can decide to ignore or neglect some alternatives; I will always be unaware of many; I can take action to close some of them to me forever, but I cannot choose to be unfree; I cannot choose to refrain from choosing. We notice that it is unlearned. I can refine my ability in selecting among some possibilities; experience teaches me to stand aside from many events. My discrimination may be improved and altered, but the capacity is innate. We can imagine also that it is unrestrained. Had I no environment, had I not to live among things and persons, nothing could interfere with the satisfaction of my wishes, and nothing would be available for their fulfillment. There could be no limit upon my choosing; hence there would be no occasion for choice; nothing does not create alternatives. Every person's environment is constantly frustrating his desire to choose, but this inhibition is necessary to his practical freedom; without environment no events would be presented to him.

At this presumed metaenvironmental level, freedom is not a skill to be learned, practiced, improved, and utilized or withheld upon volition. It is not optional either in its existence or in its exercise; it will not be increased or diminished by wish or labor. I can decide to become a pianist; I can work to develop and enhance my ability; and I can on occasion decline to perform. But I will not refuse to be free, or alter my potential to be so. Taken alone, this capacity seems inherent, irresistible, and unqualified; but it is not a separate faculty; it has no existence unto itself; it is entirely a process of more basic attributes. Choice is simply intellect, guided by preferences that are fundamentally emotional, working on environment. The power to choose is this competence either acting or awaiting options; abstracted, it is all potentiality, without limit and without opportunity.

This is the process, latent or active, that necessarily underlies and supports free acts. Granted its reality, each human is bound and privileged to pick and thread his way among and about the impossibilities and inevitable events of his physical environment and the coercions and impingements of his society and its members. Granted its reality, he is free in the only manner that a human can be, partially. Subject to social pressure and the actions of persons, he is free to select among avoidable possibilities.

Granted this, social control is a tenable concept;

obedience and disobedience are actual; we can have democracy, if we can sustain it, and anarchy for a few days, and tyranny for nearly any period; restrictions are not chimeric; interferences are not imposters; and customs can be honored, changed, ignored, and forgotten. Life is largely as we presume to know it, much as we think it to be. Choice is real.

THIS WE ALL FEEL and all believe and, though contradiction is blatant in scattered bursts of intentional dogmaticism, all do plainly live by. But it is faith, not fact. Attempts to support the belief result at best only in its restatement, references to the basic, inevasible, existential feeling that we cannot avoid choice; at worst, in fervent wishing. No proof can be adduced. Having acted, I cannot prove that I could have done otherwise by so doing in the present. Could I repeat the first instance, I might have an interesting demonstration, but that one is beyond reach; I cannot act in the past. I show only that which was done in each of two events, what I did the first time and what I did the second. That either could have been different than as it was can never be established. Neither is re-creatable; the retrieval of time is not one of the possibilities. I can state my faith, but the faith yields no verification; the facts go not beyond it. We know what we believe. The language is full with evidence. We speak of requesting and granting, of obedience and refusal, of pride and forbearance, of cruelty, abstinence, shame, repentance, virtue, punishment, vanity, mercy, and praise. The list is only started. Hundreds of these words are in daily use, and each tells of the faith that volition is real. We know what we believe, but perhaps it is all illusion.

Throughout history, religionists have been en-
thused and insistent to tell us that their God is omnipotent. They have these many centuries boasted,
threatened, and pleaded that we ought behave in accord with the principle that God is the source of every
behavior, to believe that God is the author of all belief,
to choose the faith that God is the maker of every
choice. And they have further instructed us that if we
do not do so, the All-Mighty, who is not only All-
Mighty but also All-Merciful and All-Just, will be
harsh with us. Never mind that they contradict themselves; they do that incessantly; it is their greatest
strength. But if they are accurate in the one respect, if
this part of their recital is true, the contradiction is not
their doing. Neither is their apparent duplicity, obvious disbelief, and wondrous faith their responsibility. There can be nothing that is any person's doing if
the basic fact of reality is an omnipotent Deity. Perhaps there is such—all-powerful, not as doctrine, not
as slogan, not as a crutch, not as means of frighting
children and sinners, but in fact; and not potentially,
but actually. Suppose it is true.

Now we come hard against determinism. For this
faith, freedom is but the folly or the necessity of a misled mind. The only referent of the word is an idea, and
here reference ends; the idea is the last of its line. No
reality lies behind it; the only fact is the fact of faith.
If the human were not a sentimental fool, he would
know better. At least, so it is occasionally said. But if
determinism is the fact of the world, every sentimental fool is such by necessity, and he will never know
other than as he does save it be imposed upon him.
Here we have the commitment, not that there are no

events that appear to involve social coercion and the lack of it, not that we are without occasions which appear to present possibilities and impossibilities, but that these are not what they seem. There is no denial of events, life is filled with them; the denial is that we participate therein, except as does a stone or a tree. Happening as is required, in each detail exactly as it must, is every flight of a bird, every drifting of a leaf in the still air, every movement of grass in the wind, every swirl of snowflakes in a storm, every cry of a wolf against the cold mountain, every smile of a woman, every prayer of a child, and the shifting of any stone in the edge of any surf. All is determined. The world's every event is inevitable.

II

THERE ARE TWO PRINCIPAL THEORIES of determinism. Only one is God-based. We begin here, with the system called foreordination.

At commencement, God made the plan, the universal, comprehensive, thorough creation of every event from beginning to end. Elements and weeds, planets and suns, protons and organisms, amoebae and humans, have henceforward done and will forever do as they must. The universe and all its members, every being, particle, and aggregate, in its every event, obeys the Divine Command.

Totality is the only possibility. Each occurrence, no matter how insignificant it may seem, must be irrevocably bound. Any free act could void the plan. If, as we often hear, my death is prescribed, that I will die when and only when my time comes, and if this means other than that I will not be dead until I die, I am protected until that time. Hence, the universe must be held in order; no part of it may interfere. I am immune, not to injuries that may be required of me, but to death until the plan brings my end. Further, my birth was necessary, not in even the most minor respect accidental—my particular ovum, no other—my one sperm, not one of its mates. My time can come only if I am born, not some other son or daughter of my parents, not someone who would otherwise be my sibling or my half-identical twin, but me. My parents and every other ancestor through all generations, human and pre-human, conscious and nonconscious, vertebrate and invertebrate, if such there were, must have been preserved to the point of passing at exactly the right time the exactly requisite genetic inheritance, the one selected egg, the one needed sperm that necessarily won its race with the many irrelevant ones. If any of these beings had died too soon, or become infertile or impotent prematurely, or had not been in the right place at the appointed moment, or had refused copulation, or had been pregnant, or, or, or, *ad infinitum*, the chain of heredity would have been broken, and when my time came, I would be unavailable, as would all of my intended descendants and perhaps thousands of my ancestors and all of their progeny. The world would have other persons instead, strangers to the plan, interlopers disrupting the behaviors of legitimate beings, thwarting by act and omission the divine prescript, and by misfeasance and nonfeasance spreading their influence throughout the earth until the plan was negated in its every detail.

And all of this applies not just to one point in one life, that one is only as important and as insignificant as any other, but to every point in every life, human, animal, plant, and virus, and to every moment in the existence of every inanimate thing. A boulder that rolled down a mountain and stopped in the wrong position could change the world. There are no trivial events, only those that we are required to think of as such. As each is protected, so all are bound.

None of this postulated disruption can be. God is not so weak that He is unable to bring each person to his every appointment. He is not so imperceptive as to be unable to recognize the anointed spermatozoon or so clumsy that He cannot bring it to His goal ahead of all others. He is not so impotent as to permit unscheduled impotence or unwanted infertility. He is not so confused as to create an anomaly or to fail to halt correctly a falling rock or keep a leaf in its place. Foreordination is not a sloppy system; all was done at creation and set forever. God is not merely powerful; He is onmipotent.

There is an analogy to a play, though it does not go nearly far enough. The author provides the directions; the actors do as they are told. The impersonator of Hamlet says, "To be, or not to be—that is the question," but he is not perplexed; he is only following orders. The pretender to the throne of Henry IV pleads, "O sleep, O gentle sleep,/ Nature's soft nurse, how have I frighted thee,/ That thou no more wilt weigh my eyelids down/ And steep my senses in forgetfulness?" But he is probably not insomniac; even if he is, he does not intend sleep at that point; the author decreed otherwise. The pretending king will soon be shouting at his son, "Thy wish was father, Harry, to that thought." None of this is caused by the partici-

pants or their doings; they only perform it. The cause
is Shakespeare.

So it is in the Divine Play. The objects and beings
that participate do as they must. That we find persis-
tent regularity in some classes of events and decision-
based behavior in others results from the plan; we find
as we must. That persons are sometimes excited and
often calm, that they care intensely and care not at all,
that we fight and love and hate and kill, that we pray
and curse and copulate and steal, that some think religion to be good and others think it foolish, that some
think sex to be the best of life and others hold it the
worst, that some are Christian and some are Hindu,
that some are Roman and some are Lutheran, that
some hold arcane faiths in opposition to all judgment,
that some have a faith in rationality that defies all intelligence, is in every instance the work of God. There
is no reason for anger at anyone's behavior; he could
not have done otherwise. But there is full cause for
that anger; it too was required. There is no justice in
approval of any action, but there is full call for approval; that too was ordained. All that happens is determined by Command. Even the play is part of the
Play, as actual and as artificial as any other endeavor.

Here the analogy ends; fact goes far beyond it.
Control by the human playwright is severely limited.
He puts his words on paper; those who follow do as
they wish and can with them. The actor speaks in the
voice he has, not in one devised by the author. His pronunciation and enunciation are his, not entirely like
those of any other actor who might take the part. He
may in error substitute a word or phrase for the intended one. He may be forced by memory failure to
extemporize until he finds his way. Inevitably he will

interpret; and though he intend no change, each performance will be at least in details unlike any other; the playwright does not interpret through him. The actor can make deliberate changes in his part; he can substitute, omit, and interpolate. Directors make alterations, often with enthusiasm. Editors tamper. Copyists and printers make mistakes. Authors can be careless in their typing and handwriting. Early texts are lost. Often we do not know what the creator wanted to see and hear.

But the foreordained universe is subject to none of these weaknesses. Control by the Divine Playwright is absolute. His plan cannot be misread, miscopied, or mislaid. It is not written in a human language, nor in any manner; it was merely asserted, instantaneously created. An omnipotent Being does not have to labor over an accomplishment; He does not need to symbolize it lest He forget. He creates for all time by thought only. We humans and other beings, actors in God's play, speak in the voices that our Author decreed. Pronunciation and enunciation are ours only by assignment. We make no mistakes; there is no forgetting; God has no failings. There is no interpretation; we act only in that the Author acts through us. There is one right way, His way.

That which is done unto is the object of God's agent. All that moves is the receiver of God's power. All that remains at rest is sustained by Him. Every thought, every dream, each passion comes bidden. There is only one way, His way.

THUS IS FOREORDAINED DETERMINISM one of the most honored ideas the world has known. Its premise is accepted by nearly everyone who purports religiosity.

Every person is aware, or is aware of the common concern, that if he is to feel and appear pious, if he is to "believe in God," he must answer "Yes" when asked if God is All-Powerful, that this is one of the specifics always understood to be covert in the vagary "believing in God." We all know, or know of the common assent, that power is good, that fear of God is good, that power is the inciter of fear, that omnipotence is the extension of power into perfection, that Perfection is God-Like, and that God is Good. The concept is pervasive. It is cherished, revered, employed, loved, espoused, and extolled. But nobody believes it.

This is one of the conveniences of being human. Such being can reject an idea as intellectually untenable, give joyous assent to it emotionally, shield himself from recognition of the former, bestow his love and constancy upon the latter, and congratulate his righteousness in so doing. Emotional security is more important than intellectual consistency. The reverse is probably never true, though emotional assurance is often founded in a commitment to reason.

So there is much protest that belief is at home where only affection resides; it springs from offended commitment, not from violated intellect. The complainants wish they believed and therefore insist that they do. The claims of righteousness and safety are strong, but overpowering needs press in the opposite direction. The confusion usually runs somewhat as this: The sin of pride is the most striking characteristic of humans. Man is best defined as "the prideful animal," for he unceasingly presumes to elevate himself to the rank of God. He deludes himself with the pitiable notion that he makes decisions and undertakes actions. But a moment's reflection reveals that no being with so limited intelligence, with so weak a will, with so little tendency to the Good, and of such insignificance in the Universe can have even the slightest efficacy other than as tool. Every man is wholly dependent upon his Maker for whatever he may be caused to accomplish. There is but one Power in Creation.

Here we have the traditional affirmation of God's omnipotence set against the traditional assertion of man's responsibility, amid the customary assumed power of the writer to stand aside and make factual and moral judgments, the traditional attempt to have it both ways. The commitment to omnipotence is trivially attractive to those who wish to make themselves small before an irresistible force in hope of being on the winning side and is importantly needed by serious religionists as protection against the unconscious power of the merely natural and the floundering cunning of the merely human, through which the world would otherwise go awry. As the commitment is only emotional, no serious conflicts occur; it can be adored separately from every other idea and kept from harm's way. But nothing could bring greater disaster to their religion than would their believing it. He who believes must accept its consequences.

Gone for him would be sin and guilt. Humans are not accountable for the behavior of a Deity; they do not do; they are done unto. They do not interfere nor desire to interfere with the acts of an All-Mighty Being. They do and desire as is ordained, and they ascribe sin and suffer guilt as is required. Prayer, for him, would be God's praying through intermediaries unto Himself, calling upon Himself to be attentive, petitioning Himself, informing Himself, and engaging in various acts of Self-adulation. In every blasphemy, God defames Himself. In every murder, God kills. In every sexual act—adultery, incest, and every other—God is the driving force; He brings the partners together and produces their movements and feelings. We cannot have foreordained determinism with His performing only the approved acts; He performs them all. In every sin, in every crime, God brings the hands and the minds to their tasks. If man is prideful, God required it. There is but one Power in Creation.

No religionist can forbear this. He may have compelling affinity and blessed need for a God of magnificent authority that commands the quiver of each leaf of grass, the orbits of the planets, and the happy play of children, but that He commits abominations is unconscionable. It cannot be. But even if gross unsuitability be waived, as is rarely done, and all events accepted as good—regardless of their seeming, called good because God made them—grievous difficulty remains. Without sin, without morality, without guilt, and, less importantly, without worship there is no religion, only the neutral motions and sterile passions of the Play. Those who most covet omnipotence are the most damaged by it. It comes with one great gift and stays as thief.

THE COMMITTED ARE LEFT with a pair of alternatives. The one is to fall back totally into faith and accept God as the All-Everything-That-is-Good—the All-Star General, as someone has said—to assert that the world's every event is the wish of the Omnipotent Deity who nevertheless punishes sinners with simultaneously perfect justice and infinite mercy, and to explain, if the need be, that our inability to comprehend the multiple attribution of conflicting perfections is the inevitable result and sufficient proof of the weakness of our minds, but that God, being Perfect, can understand anything, no matter how inconsistent. It is a combination much honored by tradition, the typical dishonesty and foolishness without which a holy cause cannot exist, justified, if there is demand, by appeal to stupidity.

The remaining option is compromise, to exchange rigor for acceptability, a holy cause for a place to live. Something must be done, by and for persons who insist upon at least minimal rationality, to shift the burden of evil acts from God to man. This is usually accomplished by abandoning instantaneous creation, perhaps tacitly. That done, the Plan is gone, or nearly so, and Omnipotence much modified, though each can be mentioned, even invoked, as often as piety requires or convenience suggests. God no longer has all power, though we are assured that He could have if He wished to; He is omnipotent potentially. The Plan, if it has remains, is reduced to a few major points, perhaps the end of the world is example, that are arguably not dependent upon preceding details. Otherwise, God stands aside and allows his subjects the exercise of their failing hopes and unfilled talents, their hopeless loves and muddled hates, their toiling days and worried nights, and then, when it pleases Him, brings a miracle that makes all well and right again. Creation has become continuous. We have a system not of foreordination but of intervention, not of one great miracle but of many little ones. It ignores God's perfection, neglects His omniscience, tolerates His power, respects His justice, hopes for His mercy, but exalts His freedom. Now the needful human can have his sin and guilt, his morality and his worship. He can select any occurrence and call it the Will of God, if it be his comfort to do so, and otherwise enjoy and suffer his freedom in myriad choices, while praying for another miracle. It is the common way among our traditionally semireligious, but there is very little determinism in it. That has been squeezed aside to form a place for life.

III

IN CONTRAST TO FOREORDINATION, though with much the same result, is a determinism founded in nature. The former is modeled on our usual understanding of human behavior. A man makes decisions, but much is closed to him. He is limited to the avoidable possibilities, and has time, interest, and courage for only a few of these. His attempts to bring them to achievement produce varying degrees of success, ranging down to abject failure. The more powerful a man is, the greater can be his decisions, and the less their fruition is dependent upon his effort; they become the work of those whom he commands. These ideas are then pressed to Perfection and enshrined in Deity. The Divine Tyrant, being perfect, imposes his will at every opportunity for decision; not even the meanest goes untended. Because he is perfect, every one is brought to accomplishment without effort; in Perfection, decision and realization are identical. Thus, despite the assumptions with which thought began, humanity is left powerless.

Natural determinism is modeled on what we seem to know of the behavior of inanimate objects. The

Hudson River flows downhill, not because it wishes to, not because it has been commanded, but because it is liquid water; that is what liquid water does, all liquid water, everywhere. The earth moves in its orbit, not because it abhors being consumed in the sun, not because it would be lonely if it left our solar system, not because it is fond of ellipses nor because their occasional perturbations by other planets are sensually pleasing. It is a mass in relation to other masses; it always does that which any like mass would do in like conditions. Particles attract, but no one has accused them of collusion. The principle applies throughout the universe; all is perfectly ordered. Here the fundamental faith is to extend this unimpeachable physical necessity to the whole of human behavior, not only to physiology, where it seems obviously somewhat at home, but primarily to include the acts that are often, and mistakenly in this view, called volitional. At the beginning, if there was a beginning, the regularities that we call nature came to be. If there was no beginning, they have always been. These constitute the universe. No plan exists; there is no intent; there is no controlling or overseeing mind. All existence has forever been and will forever be the outworking of Universal Causality. The world is full of objects, but there is only causality.

Most basically a human is like any other body. It is bound in the same causal nexus; it responds to stimuli in the same inexorable manner. A stone rolls, a flower opens, a tree falls, a man walks, and concrete sets when caused to do so. Nature is regular; all human behavior is natural; all human behavior is regular.

Here the analogy is to a machine, the universe in

miniature and in simple. A wheel turns because a shaft turns; the shaft turns because a pulley turns; the pulley turns because a belt moves. The belt moves when another pulley turns, because a shaft turns, because a gear turns, because its mated gear turns. We could as well substitute relay switches, condensers, magnetic bits, and cathode ray tubes. It matters not whether the analogic machine is largely electronic or entirely mechanical. And so the example goes back perhaps to an electric motor, through wires, switches, transformers, and generators to, perhaps, water falling over a dam. The wheel does not choose to rotate, nor to resist; it does as it is caused to do. The gears do not resent the wear they mutually inflict upon themselves, the belt does not long to leave the machine and enjoy the freedom of independent existence; they do as they do, not in joy, acceptance, or resignation, but through cause. There are no decisions, no enthusiasms, no mistakes; only causality. Every component, whether it turns, stops, accelerates, sticks, breaks, burns, or falls to the floor, can do no other than as it does. No part of a machine is a center of will.

So it is with Universal Causality. The things that seemingly participate do only as they must. That we presume to find decision-based behavior in some classes of events is the result of unremitting regularity; we presume as we must. That we appear to deal with each other in a profuse variety of emotions, that we plan and hope and count and pray, that we speak in hatred, anger, falsity, and truth, that some think science the only means to knowledge and others call that knowledge trivial, that some look for causes and some look for omens, that some call for facts from observation and others call upon oracles for guidance, that some have faith in reason and some decry all faith is in every event and in precise degree the one necessary effect of stimuli that were necessarily presented; they too were caused. Disapproval and commendation are without rational basis, but this is irrelevant, rational basis is foreign to the world. All that happens are effects that were prefigured in foregoing occurrences, and then become causes of effects which grow therefrom. Even the machine is part of the Machine, as natural and as necessary as any other event.

Here the analogy ends; its reach, too, is far too short. A contrivance is ever in need of help. It must be repaired, oiled, cleaned, and adjusted. Almost never does it perform as well as we would like or think it should. It must be tended, started, stopped and seemingly even prodded, patted, kicked, or treated with deference. But Universal Causality has no defects. Replacement parts do not exist; none can be used. It never breaks nor wears. It cannot be stopped, tended, cleaned, or adjusted; maintenance is not possible. We do not judge its performance; it does as it must, perfectly so. We make superficial alterations in objects and aggregates; these too are caused and have their effects, and have no influence upon causality.

An affinity for science is plain throughout; it is both conventional and deliberate, but the relationship is associative, not inherent. Through many years, the idea drew inspiration and respectability from a hoped-for identity with classical mechanics, but despite common presumption and superficial appearance, it is not a scientific theory. It has no connection unique with any physical science or version thereof and is undam-

aged by theories that view the world differently than
did early modern physics. These, old and new, can
properly be mentioned in metaphor but are otherwise
irrelevant. As literality they have no more importance
than the occasionally offered pronouncements that
whereas Newton's infinite universe provided human
freedom, Einstein's curved space precludes it, or that
through the work of Heisenberg, we are saved from the
chains of celestial mechanics, a few examples among
many of the human penchant for taking the latest intellectual success, or even unfounded innovation, to
be the explanation of everything. Though this commitment is an assertion of determinism in human af-
fairs and elsewhere, it is not in the scientific sense a
deterministic theory. To be such would require of it a
specificity and predictive value that it makes no pretense toward. It is a philosophic statement concerning
human behavior, an affirmation of faith. Its science is
an object of approval, not a practice. Its determinism is
preferential, not technical.

MUCH OF THE FOREGOING is equivocal on the status of
thought and emotion. It vacillates between they are
and they are not. Because these "mental events"—
whatever they are, perhaps nonevents—are embarrass-
ing to many of the faithful, ambivalence is typical of
the position. Here the approval that its adherents have
for empirical research is the most obvious. A very few
of them wish to think scientifically about human behavior; the others enjoy feeling scientific about it.
Hence, they prefer that the doings of humans be fully
open to observation. Science can function directly
only with that which is available to sensation, only

with empirical knowledge. Otherwise it must depend, with uncertainty and discomfort, upon inference from such knowledge. The reverse is not available; that would be to project from an unknown. The existence of a planet can be inferred from perturbations in the orbits of other bodies, but no astronomer will be satisfied until he has dependable reports of its being seen in telescopes or other such instruments. Thoughts and emotions do not lend themselves to this process; they are in principle unobservable. Uranus is an empirical object that was for the time beyond vision; circumstances changed. Thoughts are not contingently beyond sensual apprehension; they are nonempirical. The universal presumption seems to be that they are permanently unavailable to observation.

There follows the necessity of deciding what to do with, how to minimize, in the extreme, how to dispose of these parts of experience which on any other attitude are conspicuous, consequential, pervasive, and unavoidable. Most simply, three views are possible. One alternative is to assert their existence and admit their integrality in the causal nexus. But this is unsatisfactory because it permits overt behavior to be produced by causes and to produce effects that are nonempirical. Every event is strictly caused, but knowledge is limited and irresolute. We can never know when an event has an unknowable cause. We can never know when the only useful procedure would be the impossible one of deriving the perhaps potentially knowable from the unknowable. We can never know when the invisible man has readjusted the machine.

Another possibility is to restrict thoughts and emotions to being effects only, never causes. Each

is produced but never produces; it is the last of its
line. They become a superfluous fringe of action, real
enough perhaps, if anyone cares, but unimportant. All
causes are empirical; the periphery of wasted effects
can be ignored. We have all heard it: "A man does not
run because he is afraid; he is afraid because he runs."
The running is caused; it produces fear. The fear produces nothing; it is effect only. The running ceases
when the runner is caused to run no more; then fear is
discontinued. To call a nonempirical event cause is to
mistake a shadow for the substance which stopped the
light.

But the illustration goes only a short part of the
way; it is a good aphorism that is often misleadingly
presented as fact. It does not explain how a man running before a bear is more frightened than is the leader
of a race who runs before his friends. It neglects that a
person can be fearful standing quietly at the edge of a
city's quiet street and secure when running rapidly because running is fun. I was once told that I could not
think to close a door until I had made an overt move
to do so. But if this were true, I would think not of
closing the door but only of the first overt move. Asking someone to close a door would then be impossible,
as would my thinking to use this example. The principle here is better, however, than are the friendly elu-
cidations that make it look bad. They go astray in pos-
tulating an empirical event gratuitously called cause
and casually specifying a carelessly selected, nonempirical response to it. This is not only foolish sur-
plusage but on principle impossible. We cannot scientifically know nonempirical effects. All that we can
know is that they are whatever they are, if they are.
But as they cannot be known, there can be no place for

them in an idea that wishes to associate itself with empirical study. Which brings us to the third alternative.

Now the so-called mental and emotional states are banished; they are beyond notice and beyond concern. They cannot be studied; they can have no influence upon that which is studied; and though an occasional nonspecific, disparaging opinion may be permitted, even encouraged, in idle conversation, for its support of doctrine, nothing serious can be said of them. Persons who design airplanes do not study the social structures of bees and ants, mining engineers do not take account of data on the sale of violins, the captains of great ships do not look to maps and charts of Nebraska's local roads, and scientists of human behavior are likewise not diverted by irrelevance. Neither physicists, astronomers, chemists, nor behaviorists concern themselves with phantasms and apparitions. The nonempirical states thus become a superfluous and barren accompaniment to corporeal events. That the one seems to parallel the other is an interesting coincidence, but it cannot be explained. That as my hand makes these representations on paper I seem to have the words in mind is beyond comprehension. It could as well be otherwise. Why do I not regularly think of food as my hand writes words? Or the thoughts could be entirely random, making a right turn in an automobile one time, pruning a tree the next. It could as well be so; the hand is moved by cause. There is no reason why alleged thinking should proceed with that which appears on paper. It is unexplainable—surprising in an idle way, but a mystery. I could speculate about it, but I cannot say anything descriptive.

The only remaining step, this for the least secure,

is to declare thought and passion to be without existence. They are not an ornamental fringe of action nor
an unrelated annoyance; they are imaginary. We tend
to suppose them actual; but as thought is unreal, sup-
positions and imaginings concerning thought and
emotion are also nonexistent. Only he who loves that
which he hopes to reject can go so far. He looks upon
beloved commonsense reality, his unquestioned support in his every nondoctrinaire moment, and says,
"Begone; you do not exist." It is a harshness that runs
more before doubt than before courage.

But be any of this as it may, regardless of how the
equivocation is temporarily or permanently settled or
put aside, it is without effect upon the ease with which
the faith can be maintained. No matter what the ad-
justment made, anything that is recognized to exist
moves, changes, and has its being by cause. All that
occurs is produced by regularity. Every human act is
the result of universal causality. There is only one way,
the natural way. No part of the Machine is a center of
will.

SO NOW WE HAVE another blessed term. Natural causality seems as desired by some as foreordination is the
need of others. And even the urge to spread the faith is
much the same. We are often instructed that we ought
act upon the principle that every act is caused, that we
ought accept the truth that there is no choice, that if
we do not believe that rational condemnation is without reality we can rationally be condemned. Apparently the instructee is thought to be of limited understanding, and the instructor capable of reconciling any
conflict. These faithful, too, hope for the comfort of an

oscillatory commitment. They strive for is and is not, while interposing an emotional barrier to preclude either's criticizing the other. Universal determinism is praised, esteemed, flaunted, and invoked; but though sacred to many, it is believed by none. Foreordinationists are not alone in their enjoyment of the convenience of being human.

A standard confusion occurs when one of the committed explains, probably in scholarly or sermonlike style, that some person widely disparaged for his abominable behavior could not have done otherwise, that human doings are caused, not chosen, that any person in like circumstances would have performed the same acts in indistinguishable manner; and then, when this doctrine is treated with insufficient respect or when punishment is decreed upon the offender, cries out in shock and disgust against the impure who ignorantly, perversely, or in evil choose badly.

But he who believed would accept the consequences. If every act is caused, ought is always irrelevant; we act as we must, without ever an exception. If there is no choice, ought is a fool's demand in every instance, save there are no fools; we behave as we must, every time. Rational condemnation is impossible for every person always, not alone by those whose doctrinal conformity is in question or whose conversion is sought. There is no responsibility, not just for a favored few nor for the favored many, but for any person at any instant. Nobody is responsible for any act, not the criminal, not the policeman, not the prosecutor, not the juror nor the judge, neither the warden nor the guard. Nobody is ever rationally accountable. There is only futility in attempting to protect the helpless murderer from the vicious policeman; the latter is not vicious, he too is helpless. There is only mindlessness in accusing the lenient judge of loosing the malevolent criminal too soon upon the hapless public; the one is not lenient, the other is not malevolent, they too are hapless. Accusations and attempts are not possible. The world proceeds by cause, not by volition. There is never an acceptance; there is never a rejection; there is never a chosen word nor a chosen glance; neither an avoided risk nor an offer of help. We have only the vacant movements of the unconscious Machine, of which we are the misled members. There is but one power in the universe, the power of Nature.

But so strong is the need to call affection belief that occasionally we come upon even such as this: Behavioral science is analogous to physics and chemistry; they use the same methods and strive for the same results. The purpose of psychology is the prediction and control of human activity, just as the goal of physical science is the knowledge necessary to human manipulation of another class of natural occurrences. Behavior is regular; the one stimulus, or set of them, always produces the same act, simple or complex. It is the necessary result, in its every detail, of generating circumstances, a process that may be studied through observation. The investigator must find an apparent regularity and state it. He must test his statement and refine it. If after exhaustive work consistence seems to be found and clearly described, he may offer a scientific law. Thereby, a set of cause-and-effect statements that will systematize perceptions and give direction to behavior now left to mysticism, chance, and fancy is possible of attainment. It will someday be formulated. With these facts available, the skilled behaviorist will be knowledgeable to select and present stimuli that will unerringly produce a chosen and predicted behavior. Because all events are caused, control will be potentially as good as knowledge permits. Complete knowledge would bring the theoretic possibility of total control.

Statements such as this imitates are never attempts to provide formal philosophic bases for empirical study and are only incidentally held before us in furtherance of the investigation of human activity. Their recitations, in outline, of the process of science are intended for the weight of its dignity, for their hoped-for evangelic effect. But consider the basic premise. Be it believed, science is declared impossible; all of its activities are destroyed by the decree that its practitioners are unable intelligently to attempt the separation of relevance from irrelevance, unable to choose among hypotheses, ineffectual to derive rational conclusions, and incompetent to base their statements on their alleged findings. Science is not as it purports to be if its laws grow from cause but not from evidence, if they are stimulated rather than logically inferred. If its statements are nonrational, we have no reason to respect them; reason is not operative here. We are only caused to accept or reject that which cause puts forward. Conversely, though we hear it only by implication, the claim is not legitimate that scientists are excused in some of their acts from the causality that applies universally to all other beings. We cannot presume them to be as medieval priests who were anointed to perform certain tasks directly for the Supreme Power. Nature grants no dispensations, neither does it ordain acolytes.

He who believed would believe it whole. There

can be no control of beings who are only caused, by those who too can never choose; all are bound alike. There is no mysticism to defeat, no chance to tame; there is no fancy to be replaced. These occur only in our bounden or unbased imaginings; all are superfluous or compelled alike. Experimental psychology cannot be maintained on the commitment that its investigators cannot think, that they respond only inevitably to causes, just as do the ordinary humans who are their subjects, nor, at contrariety, on presumption that they are intermittently unnatural. Science is not carried on by incorporeal spirits, but if such a study of what the uninstructed call volitional behavior is to be possible, only such beings can accomplish it. Only they could be free of the determinism that is declared by this commitment to be the content of intended study. The persons who assert the most serious need of universal determinism are the most aggrieved by it. They tell of a science, and are offered a void.

THE SYSTEM IS CLOSED; no path leads beyond. Temporary escapes are not possible. All is within, and without alternative. That there is a feel of religion to it is not surprising. It is an extreme position and therefore immediately suspect, which always creates a desire for faith. And its occasional use in support of other ideologies influences the need for passionate certainty by enlarging the base of hidden doubt. Further, universal causality is often the first response and troubled repose of persons in struggle to reject religion, who are clinging firmly to the old affections while resolutely tearing away. If the omnipotent God has been important to such a person, he may put an all-causing Nature in its place and maintain the substance while changing its name. He can then demonstrate and proselyte his new freedom from faith, and his newly found faith, and his unchanged commitment. Any alternative to religion takes on a religious quality. The convert may have to cross the street, but he does not have to leave home. The only way to be done with religion is to abandon it, not to substitute for it.

A supernaturally tinged naturalism that purports the impossibility of humans holding any control of their doings, and which is believed by no one, is not of operational use to humanity. A spuriously presumed scientific basis which if taken seriously would destroy experimentation and prohibit control is of no value to the enterprise. The worth of the attitude is emotional; many find it attractive and supportive. But this from a theory that tends to distain emotions as being either trivial or fictitious is at least suspect. It needs help, but a small amount will do. The problem is only over-extension, the application of an entirely good, even unavoidable, idea beyond its competence. If we believed that trees, molecules, winds, ovaries, planets, spores, rivers, chairs, electrons, photons, gall bladders, and tectonic plates acted from choice, science would be a ridiculous idea. If they did so choose, meticulous investigation and our most casual interaction with common events would be impossible. What we think we know is obvious. We believe that most objects are caused only, that every motion of each is entirely regular. Thus we develop expectations that allow us some control of events. But to extend this limited and useful commitment to encompass all of human activity destroys every advantage that the fact or idea gives us. If we too are only caused, we have no expectations, only inevasible responses.

Which minute distinctions can most helpfully be made, where the careful lines can best be drawn, may be argued for centuries; but the principle is clear. There can be no science if there is no choice; there is no science if there are no minds. The necessity is to abandon pretense and admit belief. Tacitly, and covertly at worst, this is commonly done; humans are often not so foolish as they wish and try to be. Amid threats to survival and drives to accomplishment, reality can slip by doctrine unnoticed.

Belief is that causality is real but less than universal; only this comports with our behavior, and only this is useful. Much of experience is regular, but part of it is intellectual and volitional. A science of the former is attainable by the latter; that which is rational can investigate scientifically that which is patterned by cause. So conceived, natural determinism continues in the service of man and remains a functional idea, as it is and always has been for him who would reach for a rock or search for food, predict the time of sunrise or climb a hill, isolate a virus or set a broken leg, or design a bridge, understand the speed of light, or rock a child to sleep. But as the universal master of all, it only tempts veneration, and is otherwise ignored.

ONE POINT REMAINS. The terms 'chance' and 'random' often enter this context, usually with the appearance of being synonymous antonyms of 'cause', 'caused', 'determined', and 'determinism', and on presumption that the concept they present is the only alternative to each of those offered by the latter terms. An event that is not caused is deemed necessarily random, or "merely" chance. Hence, freedom is by definition randomality, and a free act is a chance event. The most basic of this problem I leave to another opportunity; it is only peripheral here. But the one point is needed and is immediately clear; even on the most radical definition, to be random, if such is possible, is one way to be unfree. There is no cause in it, but neither is there choice. If on this commitment human behavior is random, none of it is the doing of humans; if any occurrence in a person's activity is in this sense chance, in that occurrence he does not control himself. Whatever happens is, though perhaps not was, inevitable. But whether the polarity of chance and cause is dichotomous, continuous, or unthinkable, it is not solitary; the possibilities are not thereby exhausted. To be uncaused is not to be uninfluenced, to be unpersuaded, to have no goal or motive, or to be without intellect, experience, or memory. From these, alternatives arise; they fill the void that is the absence of cause. To shout, "Stop," to a man who is falling from a high roof is not efficacious, but to call to him who approaches the brink may have effect. A free act is subject to influence; it is neither random nor caused.

IV

THE TWO DETERMINISMS have far more in common than their common term requires. They are rich in the same emotions. Natural causality has for many decades done for a few what foreordination has over countless centuries done for many; it has helped them to feel virtuous. The latter makes them feel religious; the former inspires them to feel scientific. Neither offers a description of life nor a guide for living; none is intended. Living it is not expected; asserting it is the need. They are repositories of faith, important means of being in style. Emotional security is their common purpose. Claimants to the contrary are often heard, but they are judged by how they live, not by what they say. No one so behaves for more than a few minutes. To speak is easy; so to live the assertion of determinism as to make the speech believable is never accomplished. Doctrine encourages pretense, but pretense is all that life permits.

Fact, though, there is not. We have only the devout and the prosaic faiths, those held in hostility to belief, tending toward fervency, denunciation, and worship, and those that are belief, held not in opposition to but in the absence of knowledge, so calm that no one seems to care. If determinism is our life, our every affirmation of it, our every rejection, is irrelevantly true or false but importantly inevitable. If determinism does not so weigh upon us, if it is not the source of every act, our informal and unintentional inference from experience, our common belief that we do often choose, is true. But the truth is beyond our knowledge. All is faith; there is no fact.

Upon this unavoidable and never rejected, though easily and often denied, belief many other goods depend. Choice is at the base of every social value we have known. It is necessary to avoidable possibilities, interferences among persons, and demands within society, to democracy, science, progress, morality, and religion—all that is of merit to Western culture, or to any other. Without choice, there is no tyranny nor anarchy, no authority nor obedience, no art, magic, mysticism, preservation, nor destruction—nothing that any society prizes, nothing that is of social worth to persons. Else there remain only inevitable events and their resultant pleasures and pains, the personal satisfactions and frustrations that are fixed upon us, required by the superior force. All other is façade, only the appearance of man's participation in his life, his society, his world. Thus we are full slaves to God's plan, puppets on the strings of Divinity, or bits of matter full-subject to matter's regularity.

But all the social goods, and evils too, are safe in theory, because choice is safe within belief. Contradiction will always be; ever will we hear that every occurrence is the will of God, and that we should therefore all devote ourselves to prayer; and perhaps that we ought never punish behavior, because behavior is always caused. But such confusions are little more than demonstrations of the obvious. Each lapse emphasizes the distinction between that which the speaker wishes to believe and that which he thinks he knows; it falls between his certainty and his intermittent hope. Life requires the faith that choice is real.